THE

POPULAR

FRONT OF

CONTEMPORARY

POETRY

ANTHOLOGY

First Published by Apples & Snakes 1992

Apples & Snakes
Unit A11
Hatcham Mews Centre
Hatcham Park Mews
London SE14 5QA
Tel: 071 639 9656
Fax: 071 639 9650

Holt J., Sept. '93
821.914

ISBN: 0 9518881 0 2
A catalogue record for this book is available from the British Library

Acknowledgements

Edited by Paul Beasley for Apples & Snakes
Designed and Typeset by Bee Gittins
Cover design by Bee Gittins from the Apples & Snakes banner by Steve Lobb
Printed by Angel Press

Apples & Snakes gratefully acknowledges the support of Greater London Arts / London Arts Board in the production of this book, and the London Boroughs Grants Committee and Arts Council of Great Britain for their support in other areas of its work.

F OREWORD

This book celebrates 10 years of Apples & Snakes. Set-up at a time when a multitude of energies were laying siege to the Ivory Tower that was 'British Poetry', Apples & Snakes was fired on an original brief to promote poetry as a popular and exciting medium and as a vital community and cross-cultural activity.

In that 10 years Apples & Snakes has founded what is widely acknowledged as the most important platform in the U.K. for poetry in performance - presenting a programme of events, festivals and tours - and a parallel educational programme - which has changed the very nature and public perception of poetry for good.

For a decade Apples & Snakes has provided a forum for the creative exploration of a broad cultural / social / political agenda - embracing issues of class, race, gender and sexuality - and a launch pad for wave after wave of stylistic innovation - including the now commonly invoked 'performance poetry'- taking in jazz, dub, rap, rock, theatre, choreography and cabaret to create a popular movement in poetry that is gathering mass and momentum.

This book features 50 of the 100's of poets with whom Apples & Snakes has worked through this time - poets whose work has reanimated the expressive and social force of living word forms, both oral and literary - who through their direct engagement with audiences all over the U.K. have created a new public for poetry - bringing it back into the booming heart of popular culture.

This book samples the quality and diversity of work produced over this time, but is no retrospective - representing both known and new names, and the first British publication of almost 2/3rds of the work included.

Looking back - Apples & Snakes is where poets reawakened to the full-bodied poten-

FOREWORD

tials of poetry, especially by putting the accent back on the voice - reactivating dynamics that are reverberating through the media - demonstrating an aesthetic which breaks down the walls of silence and bridges the distances yawning between poetry and people.

Looking forward - this movement has created the conditions for the realisation of infinite possibilities - as poetry rediscovers itself at a point where all cultural forms converge and diverge.

Paul Beasley
for Apples & Snakes

CONTENTS

CONTENTS

CONTENTS

CONTENTS

CONTENTS

Riding On De Riddym

riding on de riddym a we time
sorting out the questions on we mind
wedda hustling on street corner
or white collared in de corridor
we own images we seeking to define

de cap couldn't fit
de muse pack er grip
move outa Egyp
now she roving like a gypsy
cause accomodation
it nat easy
an too much craftis reachin er by telephone
an she didn' waan go mental all alone
so she can change up er french line image
an she skankin down de frontline raw
meetin metaphors mongs King Tubby's hi fi
tappin out a timin mongs de hip hop an de jive
jumpin de A train to a Harlem song
whe words flying like bullets
baratta strong
realising how bored she had been
all long

now we riding on de riddyms a we time
sorting out de questions on we mind
wedda hustling on street corners

or white collared in de corridor
we own images we seeking to define

de Latin wasn' hip
pentecostal tongue lick we lip
light we wid poetic flame
mongs de kumina, de shango,
de ettu an de balm
everyone weh hear can understan
in de yard, in de park,
in de football stan'
de muse now say she coming live
she don' like how er influence get prioritise
wid de five percent a light demself
an aestheticise
an de majority don' even realise
dat is dem retain de culture dat keep er alive
so she jump offa de page
jump up on de stage
mongs de d.j. an de dancehall
de jazz, de blues, de grays,
poetry now bus out a de stays

an we riding on de riddym a we time
sorting out de questions on we mind
wedda we hustling on street corner
or white collared in de corridor
we own images we seeking to define
an de muse sey to tell yuh
she having a rapsiraggaraving time

Red Rebel Song

is lang time
i waan sing dis song
      sing it loud
      sing it long
      no apology
      no pun
jus a raw fire madness
a clinging to de green
a sargasso sea

is years
of ungluing Iself
from de fabric of lust
dat have I
in a pin-up glare

years
of trying to buil
de trust

lang time I waan
free Iself
from de white black question
from de constant hairpulling
breadfruit baiting
coconut shaking

hypocrisies
   of I skin
       have nutten to do
but lie dung
pon Massa bed
outside
field slave sing loud
       to open sky
hear dem own ancestral echo
       in de wind
I een de house
tie up wid apron
between bedroom
where white mammy
practising piano
an kyan quite
reach de blues
an de kitchen
where black mammy
reign supreme
where mi soul
     steam out
smell like fresh clothes
       wash wid roses soap

lang time
my song lock up tight
eena mi troat

like if a ever open mi mout
                              jus to breathe
de roar would shake dis eart
an matterkine
                    split
an microchip   cho   jus fly

yes!
I feel like I
sitting on a time bomb
an I kyan get angry
fah yuh would see
mountain quake
an certain bway
weh ah entertain
delegation after delegation
an still kyan solve
a likkle irrigation
shoulda jus get lick
an stamp pon a envelope
wid no return address

                    nuff sista an bredda like I
red wid anger
kyan explode
            is I an I leg split
            open
cross dis sea

of hatred an indifference
       tekkin injection after injection
fi cure di madness an pull we foot togedda
      is I an I
did climb mountain
an try carry a cloudful
a tears
pon we head
so Noah wouldn't haffi
buil a nex ark
fi save we fram de waters

    I is de red rebel
woman
    holding eart
north pole to
south
    tropical
    wet
heating whole continents wid a
    rain forest intensity
let go eida side
    is to lose part of I
      bridge
    over troubled water lay
some loving on I now
    watch I
  painted halfbreed
  centrespread
   I nah
      tek no abuse fram eida direction

I is
red ribba
foot shape outa country clay
Madda
of white children red children an black
who!

lang time
I wanna sing dis song
sing it loud
sing it long
no apology
no pun
jus a rawfire madness
a clinging to de green
a sargasso sea

I release Iself
from de promise
of eternal compromise
from de bed of rapists
black or white
from page 3
from
cho
if I waan gi yuh piece
is mine
free
no apology

lang time I reaping
                byblows
                peepshows
                whoknows
                wat amount of dose
I live it
I feel it
I sing it
                it don't mek life no easier
                but it sure don't mek it wrong

I is de free christian
who know Jah
de one who roam
an come home
I is de red rebel
woman
accepting I madness
declaring I song
nah siddung eena attic
tek no fire bun
I singing it loud
I singing it long
think seh I done
well
I jus a come
        I I I own rainbow
        I I I own song

Bagpipe Muzak,
Glasgow 1990

When A. and R. men hit the street
To sign up every second band they meet
Then marketing men will spill out spiel
About how us Glesca folk are really *real*
(Where once they used to fear and pity
These days they glamorize and patronize our city-
Accentwise once they could hear bugger all
That was not low, glottal or guttural,
Now we've 'kudos' incident'ly
And the Patter's street-smart, strictly state-of-the-art,
And our oaths are user-friendly).

It's all go the sandblaster, it's all go Tutti Frutti,
All we want is a wally close with Rennie Mackintosh
    putti.

Malkie Machismo invented a gismo for making whiskey oot
    o' girders
He tasted it, came back for mair, and soon he was on his
    thirders.
Rabbie Burns turned in his grave and dunted Hugh
    MacDiarmid,
Said: It's oor National Thorn, John Barleycorn, but I doot
    we'll ever learn it...

It's all go the Rotary Club, it's all go 'The Toast tae The

Lassies',
It's all go Holy Willie's Prayer and plunging your dirk in the
    haggis.

Robbie Coltrane flew Caledonian MacBrayne
To Lewis...on a Sunday!
Protesting Wee Frees fed him antifreeze
(Why God knows) till he was comatose
And didnae wake up till the Monday.

Aye it's Retro Time for Northern Soul and the whoop and
    the skirl o' the saxes.
All they'll score's more groundglass heroin and venison
    filofaxes.
The rent boys preen on Buchanan Street, their boas are made
    of vulture,
It's all go the January sales in the Metropolis of Culture.

It's all go the PR campaign and a radical change of image -
Write Saatchi and Saatchi a blank cheque to pay them for
    the damage.

Tam o'Shanter fell asleep
To the sound of fairy laughter
Woke up on the cold-heather hillside
To find it was ten years after
And it's all go (again) the Devolution Debate and pro...
    pro... proportional representation.
Over pasta and pesto in a Byres Road bistro, Scotland
    declares hersel' a nation.

Margo McDonald spruced up her spouse for thon Govan By-
Election
The voters they selectit him in a sideyways *left* defection,
The Labour man was awfy hurt, he'd dependit on the X-
fillers
And the so-and-sos had betrayed him for thirty pieces of
Sillars!

Once it was no go the SNP, they were sneered at as 'Tory'
and tartan
And thought to be very little to do with the price of Spam
in Dumbarton.
Now it's all go the Nationalists, the toast of the folk and the
famous
- Of Billy Connolly, Murial Gray and the Auchtermuchty
Proclaimers.

It's all go L.A. lager, it's all go the Campaign for an
Assembly,
It's all go Suas Alba and winning ten-nil at Wembley.
Are there separatist dreams in the glens and the schemes?
Well....it doesny take Taggart to detect it!
Or to jalouse we hate the Government
And we patently didnae elect it.
So - watch out Margaret Thatcher, and tak' tent Neil
Kinnock
Or we'll tak' the United Kingdom and brekk it like a
bannock.

LIZ LOCHHEAD

View Of Scotland/Love Poem

Down on her hands and knees
at ten at night on Hogmanay,
my mother still giving it elbowgrease
jiffywaving the vinolay. (This is too
ordinary to be nostalgia.) On the kitchen table
a newly opened tin of sockeye salmon.
Though we do not expect anyone,
the slab of black bun,
petticoat-tails fanned out
on bone china.
'Last year it was very quiet...'

Mum's got her rollers in with waveset
and her well-pressed good dress
slack across the candlewick upstairs.
Nearly half-ten already and her not shifted!
If we're to even hope to prosper
this midnight must find us
how we would like to be.
A new view of Scotland
with a dangling calendar
is propped under last year's,
ready to take its place.

Darling, it's thirty years since
anybody was able to trick me,

December thirtyfirst, into
'looking into a mirror to see a lassie
wi' as minny heids as days in the year'-
and two already since
familiar strangers at a party,
we did not know that we were
the happiness we wished each other
when the Bells went, did we?

All over the city
off-licences pull down their shutters.
People make for where they want to be
to bring the new year in.
In highrises and tenements
sunburst clocks tick
on dusted mantelshelves.
Everyone puts on their best spread of plenty
(for to even hope to prosper
this midnight must find us
how we would like to be).
So there's a bottle of sickly liqueur
among the booze in the alcove,
golden crusts on steak pies
like quilts on a double bed.
And this is where we live.
There is no time like the
present for a kiss.

JACKIE KAY

This Long Night

This long night talks to itself.
The dark won't listen to the sound of your name.
I reach out here - my big empty bed.
The space next to me closes in; you say something,
anything, the exact sound of your accent
falling like rain on a caravan roof.
Tell me what you want me to do.

This long night stretches into another time.
Nobody calls my name. Silence -
a thief in the back garden.
Your body, a shadow, flat under the moon.
In my sleep, I open up like a night flower.
My scent comes in the midnight hour.
You come in by the window, don't you?

This long night and I can't reach you.
Your tongue inside me slides away.
You walk through the pitch dark, slowly.
Touch the dark arm of a tree.
Your skin is a light in the garden. I wake up.
You turn in your sleep next to your marriage;
wake yourself up calling my name.

Brendon Gallacher (For my brother, Maxie)

He was seven and I was six, my Brendon Gallacher.
He was Irish and I was Scottish, my Brendon Gallacher.
His father was in prison; he was a cat burglar.
My father was a communist party full-time worker.
He had six brothers and I had one, my Brendon Gallacher.

He would hold my hand and take me by the river
Where we'd talk all about his family being poor.
He'd get his mum out of Glasgow when he got older.
A wee holiday someplace nice. Some place far.
I'd tell my mum about Brendon Gallacher.

How his mum drank and his daddy was a cat burglar.
And she'd say why not have him round to dinner.
No, no, I'd say he's got big holes in his trousers.
I like meeting him by the burn in the open air.
Then one day after we'd been friends two years

One day when it was pouring and I was indoors,
My mum says to me; I was talking to Mrs Moir
Who lives next door to your Brendon Gallacher
Didn't you say his address was 24 Novar?
She says there are no Gallachers at 24 Novar

There never have been any Gallachers next door.'
And he died then, my Brendon Gallacher
Flat out on my bedroom floor, his spikey hair,
His impish grin, his funny flapping ear.
Oh Brendon. Oh my Brendon Gallacher.

JACKIE KAY

Dressing Up

My family's all so squalid
I'm trying to put it behind
me - real typical working class
Scottish: Da beats Ma drinks it off.
I couldn't stomach it, banging

doors, turning ma music up top
blast. I told ma ma years ago. She'd
rather I murdered somebody than
that. She wasn't joking either.
Nobody gets hurt, it's not for

the image even I'm just dead
childish. Mascara I like, rouge
putting it on after powder.
I love wearing lots of layers.
Ma ma always dresses boring

No frills. See at Christmas I had
on black stockings Santa would kill
for and even Quentin Crisp would
look drab beside my beautiful
feather boa - bright fucking red.

Ma ma didn't touch her turkey
Finally she said What did I do
I know what they call you, transvite.
You look a bloody mess you do.
She had a black eye, a navy dress.

Dance of the Cherry Blossom

Both of us are getting worse
Neither knows who had it first

He thinks I gave it to him
I think he gave it to me

Nights chasing clues where
One memory runs into another like dye.

Both of us are getting worse
I know I'm wasting precious time

But who did he meet between
May 87 and March 89.

I feel his breath on my back
A slow climb into himself then out.

In the morning it all seems diffcrent
Neither knows who had it first

We eat breakfast together - newspapers
And silence except for the slow slurp of tea

This companionship is better than anything
He thinks I gave it to him.

Jackie Kay

By lunchtime we're fighting over some petty thing
He tells me I've lost my sense of humour

I tell him I'm not Glaswegian
You all think death is a joke

It's not funny. I'm dying for fuck's sake
I think he gave it to me .

Just think he says it's every couple's dream
I won't have to wait for you up there

I'll have you night after night - your glorious legs
Your strong hard belly, your kissable cheeks

I cry when he says things like that
My shoulders cave in, my breathing trapped

Do you think you have a corner on dying
Your self-pitying wretch, pathetic queen.

He pushes me; we roll on the floor like whirlwind;
When we are done in, our lips find each other

We touch soft as breeze, caress the small parts
Rocking back and forth, his arms become mine

There's nothing outside but the noise of the wind
The cherry blossom's dance through the night.

Bearing Witness

*(dedicated to James Baldwin who in his last
recorded interview said that he wanted black
writers to bear witness to the times)*

Bearing witness to the times
where it pays to sell lines
Where African thighs thrive for twenty five
and guns run with the midnight son.

Bearing witness to the days
of the blue eyed glaze
of the black eyed girl of the world
whose life depends on a contact lens.

Bearing witness to the screams
of children cut on shattered dreams,
colonialised minds lost in times
of permanent frowns and nervous breakdowns.

Bearing witness to the signs
of white sandstorms in black minds,
of waves from the west with white dagger crests
scratching the black beaches back.

Bearing witness to the hour
where maladjusted power

realigns its crimes in token signs
then perversely repents with self-punishment.

Bearing witness to the times
where we black people define
the debt yet to be paid, you bet
I'll be rhyming the fact when I witness that.

Boiling Up

Can you spread me lightly on this street?
I would like to blend in.
If butter and bread can do it, so can I.

Will you sprinkle me softly in this hotel?
I would like to blend in.
If chicken and seasoning can do it, so can I.

(The store detective is either trying to
strike up some kind of meaningful relationship with me
or I've got a box of jelly babies stuck to my left ear.)

Could you drip me into this club?
I would like to blend in.
If coffee and milk can do it, so can I.

(It's not a sawn-off shotgun in my inside pocket,
and that's not because I keep my machete there -

ten Regal King size, please.)

Can you grate me into this city?
I would like to blend in.
If cheese and tomatoes can do it, so can I.

Can you soak me into this country?
I would like to blend in.
If rice and peas can do it, so can I.

Brinkley Park

In the interval of each footstep a distant drunken couple laugh.
Like a lioness chewing gravel her feet crunch the speckled path,
Thinking of every memory hugging short cut she knew so well
Her mind suspended in the chimes of the 3am church bell.
As she pondered on the warmth of pillow and sheet
She slowly bent under the shadow of the willow to rub awake her sleeping
  feet

And it was cold wet and hauntingly dark
As she stepped through the bowels of Brinkley Park.

The trees, dew-slimy as the beads of sweat on the face of the killer.
The mist clinged to oak and grass, like a scene from a midnight thriller.
Yet this was a far cry from any television show,
As were her treacle tears with each life sapping blow.
Shadows ripped the grass verges into vast empty ravines,

Vast and empty enough to swallow her muffled screams.
He acted out his illness, gas to his hallucinated spark,
The day he raped Charla Leeston in the bowels of Brinkley Park.

Again another woman falls victim to the penis wrapped in barbed wire.
Again another woman withdraws seeing smoke and in fear of the fire.
Again another woman wraps herself in one piece of clothing more.
Again another woman finds the thirteenth bolt for her security door.

The Show Goes On

The arts council criteria for funding is to conform
So if they pay the revolution the revolution will perform

And if you write along the dotted line you role in this
                                                    society
Then you can pay allegiance to the notorious great race
                                                    robbery
And with a knowing glint in your eye they'll say you can
                                                    apply
Then they'll stuff your open mouths with a piece of
                                        American Pie
Saying...............

The arts council criteria for funding is to conform
And as we are paying the revolution, the revolution will
                                                    perform

And like puppets on barbed wire
We dance in this fire
And we...becoming the actresses and actors...are forgetting
the plot
Knowing so much that we needed something but not knowing
what
And we try to ignore this cynicism while stuffing our pockets
with gold
Saying, well if they give it then take it that's what I was told

But the arts council criteria for funding is to conform
Which means if they pay the revolution, the revolution will
perform

And Marcus Garvey turns in his grave seeing the liberalism he
fought
Seeing the modern day slave being sold and being bought
One slave was allocated to dance another was commissioned
to write poetry
It was an unwritten law that if we dance write sing and paint,
we will forget about our slavery
Time is being intricately fooled and we are the fools
Cause if we take a look over the chimney pots we're being
ridiculed
Yes, the revolution will be hidden for another one hundred
years
Or at least as long as governmental funding is here
And an added bonus is getting us to believe in multiculturalism

Again keeping our minds from the real situation

That the arts council criteria for funding is to conform
And if it pays the revolution the revolution will perform

Yes we are a beautiful people because through all this we still
see light
But just like the winter
The days are getting shorter
And will we know what to do in the night

Every second counts, every minute minute, every haunting
hour
This country is exerting a silent massacre
Every second counts, every minute minute, every harrowing
hour
Ask yourself and seek the answer, where is the fund for Black
power!

LINTON KWESI JOHNSON

Di Anfinish Revalueshan

now watchya mistah man
mi noh like di way yu tan
an yu tan soh too lang yu know man
a meditate yu a meditate pan di same sang soh lang?
well hear mi man:

mi naw preach
mi naw teach
mi jusa show yu
ow mi seit
caw di trute well sweet
jus like a African beat
like wen yu si whey yu comin fram
like wen yu site whichpawt yu reach
soh mi noh care if yu waan vex
ar even gwaan like yu perplex
mi a goh show yu whey mu si mistah man

yu jus siddung an folc-up like a cabbidge
like seh yu gat noh andahstandin gat no nallidge
like seh yu still noh realise seh a jus di addah day
wi chuck-awf di chokin chains af bandidge
dat in spite a di hateridge an disadvantage
dow wi slip-up an stumble pan di way
wi still reach far doun freedam street
still mindful af di minefields pan di way

soh mi a beg yu mistah man
please come out a yu shell
yu cyaan dwell inna di paas
dat laas fi evah yu know mi bredda
now dat di sun a shine brite
please come out a di doldrums a di daak nite

histri biggah dan mi ar yu yu know
time cyaan steal but it can heal
soh shake di dew fram out yu hed
wipe di cabweb fram yu face
wi gat nuff work fi dhu
far wi noh reach mount zion
yet

yes wi phudung a salid foundaeshan
fi true
an wan an two a wi well a get tru
fi true
but wi still noh bil di new jerusalem
yet

di time goin come agen
yu can bet
wen wi a goh march awn agen
yu hear mi fren
mobilise wi women an wi fren dem
agen

even di pickney dem a goh jine een
far freedam is nat noh idealagy
freedam is a human necessity
it cyaan depen pan now wan somebady
is up to each an evry wan a wi

mi naw preach
mi naw teach
mi jusa show yu
ow mi seit
caw di trute well sweet
jus like a African beat
like wen yu si whey yu comin fram
like wen yu site whichpawt yu reach
soh mi noh care if yu waan vex
ar even gwaan like yu perplex
mi jusa show yu whey mi si mistah man

ABDUL MALIK

Countdown

Time of momentum
Time of continuing momentum
Time of continuing momentum momentum
for human freedom
Time of conclusion
Time of increasing conclusion
Time of increasing conclusion conclusion
of human freedom
Time of eclipsing Socialism
Time of resetting Europeanism
Time of discerning Globalism Capitalism Environmentalism

(Refrain)

Time Year '90
Time Year count down
to the Twenty First century
HOLD ON TO HUMANITY
HOLD ON TO HUMANITY
Time Year '90
Time Year count down
down
down
down
HOLD ON TO HUMANITY
HOLD ON TO HUMANITY

Time of exhaustion
Time of continuing exhaustion
Time of continuing exhaustion exhaustion
for human freedom
Time of pollution
Time of increasing pollution
Time of increasing pollution pollution
of human freedom
Time of deranging Communalism
Time of consuming Third Worldism
Time of unleashing Racism Fascism Barbarism

(Refrain)

Time Year '90
Time Year count down
to the Twenty First century
HOLD ON TO HUMANITY
HOLD ON TO HUMANITY
Time Year '90
Time Year count down
down
down
down
HOLD ON TO HUMANITY
HOLD ON TO HUMANITY

Time of rotation
Time of continuing rotation

Time of continuing rotation rotation
for human freedom
Time of erosion
Time of increasing erosion
Time of increasing erosion erosion
of human freedom
Time of reversing Universalism
Time of revealing Materialism
Time of the hole
Time of the ozone layer
Time of the World
Time of enveloping terror

(Refrain)

Time Year '90
Time Year count down
to the Twenty First century
HOLD ON TO HUMANITY
HOLD ON TO HUMANITY
Time Year '90
Time Year count down
down
down
down
HOLD ON TO HUMANITY
HOLD ON TO HUMANITY
HOLD ON TO HUMANITY
HOLD ON TO HUMANITY

ADRIAN MITCHELL

Ten Holes For A Soldier

Two holes were the size of the holes in his ears.
They were rounded and as they opened and shut
They seemed to make a sound like sighing.

Two holes were the size of his nostrils,
Close together and dark inside
And breathing out a smell of something rotting.

Two holes were the size of his eyes
And they were trying to clench themselves
To hold back the red tears.

One hole was the size of his mouth
And it cried out
With the voice of an old child.

One hole was the size of the hole
In the end of his cock
And it was skewered by a white-hot, turning gimlet.

One hole was the size of the hole in his arse,
Small and wincing away from the light.
And it went very deep.

Petrol was poured into all his holes.
All of his holes were set on fire.

They covered his holes with a clean uniform.
They flew him home. There was a flag.
In the village he loved, they put him in a hole.

Evenings of Fire and Snow

Don't look so worried
I understand
Let me touch your forehead
With my freckled hand
Won't you sit beside me
For a little while?
It would satisfy me
Just to see you smile

> I'm transparent
> Look into me
> Look at my childish heart's
> Simplicity
> Whiteness shining
> And a crimson glow
> Heat and coldness
> Fire and snow

And if you'll allow me we will know
Evenings of fire and snow

Don't want to own you
I'm happy just to share

It's a joy to know you
Know you know I care.
Won't you let me love you
On this sunset day?
Smiling when you leave me,
I will only say -

> I'm transparent
> Look into me
> Look at my childish heart's
> Simplicity
> Whiteness shining
> And a crimson glow
> Heat and coldness
> Fire and snow

And if you'll allow me we will know
Evenings of fire and snow

JOHN AGARD

In Times Of Love

In times of love
simple things spring new life
ancient patterns weave
fresh meanings
to your fevered eyes

the sun
you never looked for in the skies
offers your skin
a flaming benediction
and the rain
once a nuisance to your day
is living drum
for warming blood
and twinning flesh

in times of love
you let the child inside of us
have its way
and learn to look for dreams
beneath the dust

Heart Transplant

No puff
no pant
check out
a heart transplant

let's swop
your heart
for mine
heart transplant
the new life line

come on baby do the heart transplant
come on baby do the heart transplant

experiment number 1
put the heart of a bird
inside a stone
meditate on that

behold
the stone sings
the stone grows wings
wondrous flight
of a common thing

experiment number 2
a medical breakthru
put the heart of your average politician

John Agard

into a common stone

behold
stones grow paranoid
stones grow suspicious of grass
stones hurl themselves into the void
the blue emptiness

alas
will stones develop a paunch

seeking the votes of God

Limbo Dancer's Memo

Chained in limbo
watch a body flow
from web of darkness
                    into light

historical memory
linking / me back
                to human cargo
                a seed of light
                in limbo

Again I say to you
you don't need to own
radio /or video

to know that they lay low
our prophets of hope
who dare voice
the suffering
            of the ghetto

I promise not to use words
like oppression / exploitation
genocide / nuclear waste
ecological suicide /
for you have heard them
so many dog-eat-dog times

But upon the wicked ones
I cast curse
as did my mother before me
mother of universe

            limb of my limb / mover of galaxy
            limb of my limb / bow of harmony

I queen of limbo
I king of limbo
world without end
will not bend
to fixed roles
of their status quo

I limbo dancer
too supple
            for their double standards

JOHN AGARD

to be / or not to be
passive / aggressive /
feminine cry / masculine cry not /
play with dolls / play with guns /
follow emotion / follow logic /

all so rigid / all so slick
but jill be nimble
jill be quick
jill dance under the limbo stick

I queen of limbo
I king of limbo
I whose knees
have spanned the Atlantic

will grant the blind ones
their commercial breaks
their sugarcoated con / trick

But rulers of the world
before you dance with me
                    you must first overthrow your ego

Rulers of the world
O hear me / take heed
           for you know / & I know / & the people know

                limousines do not bleed

chant me a tune

when you see me weak and wondering
as you sometimes will
chant me a tune

move with me across the weeping atlantic
through the blood tears death pain and hurt
through the thundering angry sighing sobbing fury
of the startled atlantic
throbbing with the pulsing pages of a story
written as footnotes to an eager quest for land

chant me a tune
move with me beyond the rattle of the chains
and watch me rise with Nanny in Jamaica
where they pulled the cup drained the sorrow
rooted out the pain
and are still seeking beneath the hope

when you see me weak and wondering
as you sometimes will
don't try to dust my story
into the crevices of time
chant me a tune

speak to me of Mary Seacole
who washed their tears
and calmed their fears

and got lost behind white nightingales
somewhere in the telling of the story

when you see me weak and wondering
chant me a tune
remind me how much
i am a part of your surviving
just as you are a part of my believing

remind me
that though i am a part of those who died
because they simply could not bear to live
i am also of those who lived
because they would refuse to die

chant me a tune
speak to me of what we have been
of what we are
of what we are creating

when you see me weak and wondering
as you sometimes will
i need you
to remind me
that i am
the oceanic roar of angry strength
that never dies
that never dies
that never will die

she was quiet

she was quiet
until you looked into her eyes
and then you thought
well, perhaps not so much quiet
as unrevealing

she was meek
moved about the kitchen
as if she would step aside
to give an ant the right of way

she was meek
until you looked into her eyes
and then you thought
well, perhaps not so much meek
as undemonstrative

she was mary the cook
who walked without moving
who talked without a voice
who looked without seeing
who listened without hearing

just another faceless person
unseeing and unseen
on the streets of London

not much was ever said of mary
and mary never had much to say
for herself at all
until, one day

you visit the cook in hospital
and she startles you to silence
by meeting your routine how are you

not with well
not with fine
not even with
well, not so well today

but by speaking of her mother
of her son in the village
of Nigeria
and of the world
as if she knew so much
not only of its pain
but also of its possibilities
made impossible

and when mary's eyes say with searching
how I am is all a part of that
you are silent now
you feel faceless, too

thank God mary says thank God thank God
that she had made some time
to visit them in the village last year
her anxious mother and her waiting son

and you had this image of mary wresting time
from those who had control of it
breaking it like the bottle
and remaking just a little piece
to suit herself, thank God

now they say that if they can find no-one
perhaps they will bury mary
in an unmarked grave
or perhaps they may even cremate mary
and scatter her ashes on a wintry English day

mary who had come to England in search of dreams
who had hoped to go home tomorrow
until the cancer that had been in her life
since yesterday

ate its wary watchful way
into her breast today
and left tomorrow
searching for another day

I wonder who will now make some time
who will find the money

MERLE COLLINS

that mary never made enough of
here in her English home

to seek and tell her anxious mother
and her waiting son

Reflecting on her granddaughter

And the little granddaughter
growing up like pothouse flower
in a England basement flat.
Growing bolder and bolder
into teenage warrior-queen
who want learn high-kick karate,
with hairstyles taking you
into twenty-first century -
a geometrical natural above her neck
to show her African-pride,
front permed-dyed, bright gold
(after all she is, Woman Of The Times)
And her girl-friend, white,
whose hair she courses into braids,
drawing her to rhythms of black,
lost in reggae, ragga, rap.

But who can keep these girls
with search-for-love inside?
Who can keep them from the hidden
side of life?
And her mother have no idea
of them sitting round,
braving spliff. Lovey with boys,
(now they into black)
and her ego hasn't yet learnt

the knack of being possessive
of her race.
And her mother prays
something would change her wildways.
Not wanting her Ophelia-like.

       Just walking..............
       in the strong and lovely balance
       of herself.

MARC MATTHEWS

U Freak Out

20th Century living is a
death BOOM - Listen
the distant moaning
the rasping clang of metal
& wear
the forgotten noise of Guns

Look
Out of a millium of Light
& Silence comes voices
Alien voices with bells
distorted from the past
muddled by the riddle of
years

Listen
the knife the fork the
plate
motors moaning like rain
in a forest night
            miles away

20th Century living is
a snake pit
films curry aspirins &
astronauts

heard in overcoats & children
voices
seen thru the sleeping
wide eyed
rubber squeaking dolls
all in the raincoat of a
room -

In the damned years
a million pistons ring
the century to a close

There are valleys outside
Hard cold grey stone
lined side by side
edge to edge
wet grey stone splashed
with the white grips of Black tyres

inside is a complicated
combination of tubes
red, grey, black tubes
moving an Army
to keep specimens
working
feel -
busy a million crawling
blood vessels

swam rub grind hold
shake the system of the
mind
further lower lower
they stretch
Wax white - eat it
burn it
it grows on finger nails
it's clear
transparent
it's panic
it melts

Look
those lines criss crossing
the golden threads of eyes
those wire webs crowding
in inner iris of shadows
finger on bone
on plastic
on page
a million piston ring
& the century of man
comes to close

The T.V.
has my head under its
arm

MARC MATTHEWS

I flap neckless on a
bed

A district of
horizontal lives
scream white faced from
the box
Box, black death bands
Brass handles spades dirt
quiet-faced priests with
fertilisers in their hands
mumble sans end sans end
DIRT DIRT DIRT A
FLOOR
the world is a floor of
Dirt to die in

20th Century is celloyde
SELL U LOID
wire light shadow
strings
ink page
mike crow phones
on   off
Red   Green
Light Shadow
a million specks
of
dark dots
white dots

light shadow
hazy shadow
wires tapes lights
strings ink page
   type type
     ribbon
tape spool
      reel
wind wind
rush rush
scatter scatter
light shadow
    focus
Light
     metal
        wire
          shadow
words
    light
shines Lines Lines
entire Lines Lines
Lines Lines
      Lines
Lines Lines Lines
        Shine
Lines Lines
      Hear see listen
as a million pistons
are ringing the human
century to a
     CLOSE!

Ian McMillan

The Er Barnsley Seascapes

1. Goldthorpe Er Seascape

Park the car. Wind
the window down. Listen.
Shanties, echoing
up the tight street

as the pitmen sing
their way from work.
The YTS lamplighter
stands, and his matches

cough out in
the well-trained wind.
He was not a clever boy at school

so all he can say is
shit, not like us
clever people, who wind
the window down to catch

the dying tradition
on our Japanese tape recorders.
Shanties, clinking like
cardboard money,

the cardboard money
they have round here.
Burns easier.
Cheaper than coal.

2. M1 Seascape Near Hoyland: Er It's A Rough Day

They huddle in their coats
and the gaffer holds his gun
but only for effect. For this
photograph I am taking, I suppose.

For the interview, the gaffer
is proud: 'We have only six more
miles of motorway to roll up
and dump in the sea' he quips.

3. Er Darfield Seascape

And the waves pound
against Clifton's shop
and Clifton's shop never closes.
On Christmas Day someone rushes in
for a pair of tights. She has
a bulging purse from Habitat
in the shape of a bath
filled with coal. Habitat coal,
silly bastard. Put it this way:
Darfield was mentioned in the Domesday Book.
Put it like this: a passing mention,

IAN McMILLAN

more of a mutter.

4. Little Houghton Seascape Er Like
British Coal
sold the house

made us live
in heads.

Great big
severed heads.

Rows of heads
overlooking the sea.

Sometimes I stand
in the eyes

and I cry.
Then I burn

the tears.
Cheaper than coal.

5. An Old Seadog Er Speaks
First it was called NCB, you'd see it
on the boats, then British Coal, on
the wharves, then they changed the name

to British A Vase of Flowers, changed all
the boats, all the wharves, all the
signs outside the pits, then they
changed it to British Very Nice
and a month later to British Smile
and they kept repainting the boats
the wharves the fish the seaweed the

6. Er From A Learned Paper About The Seascapes

Very few of er the South Yorkshire
Coastal Mining Settlements survive
in anything like their original

er state. Some have become islands,
some have sunk into the sea, some
have worked loose from the earth

and slither around the countryside
scaring er owls and other woodland
creatures. One was found in Harrogate,

a town in North Yorkshire next to
the sea. 'It had er wings' said a local,
'and was tired from much hard flying'.

7. Seaview Video, Barnsley Er Latest Offers

Barnsley is Basingstoke!   £1.00 a night.
Barnsley is Basingstoke 2!   £1.00 a night.

The Cruel Sea (Remake)	£1.00 a night.
Lost Horizon (Remake)	£1.00 a night.
Barnsley is Japan!	£1.00 a night.
Barnsley is Japan 2!	£1.00 a night.

8. Seascape Could Er Be Anywhere Round Here

Only the water, solid
and glinting. Only
the noise of the water,

and the noise of the moon
slowly deflating, and
only the noise of the stars

being sold, clinking,
keeps me awake
all day.

Ted Hughes Is Elvis Presley

I didn't die
that hot August night.
I faked it,

stuffed a barrage balloon
into a jump suit.
Left it slumped
on the bathroom floor.

Hitched a ride on a rig
rolling to New York. Climbed
into the rig, the driver said
"Hey, you're..."
"Yeah, The Big Bopper. I faked it,
never died in that 'plane crash.
Keep it under your lid."
I tapped his hat with my porky fingers.
He nodded. We shared a big secret.

Laid low a while in New York.
Saw my funeral on TV in a midtown bar.
A woman wept on the next stool but one.

"He was everything to me. Everything.
I have a hank of his hair in my bathroom
and one of his shoelaces

Ian McMillan

taped to my shoulderblade."

"He was a slob" I said.
She looked at me like I was poison.
"He was too, too big," I said.
"He wanted to be small, like
a little fish you might find in a little pond."

I needed a new identity.
People were looking at me.
A guy on the subway asked me
if I was Richie Valens.

So I jumped a tramp steamer
heading for England.
Worked my passage as a cook.
In storms the eggs slid off the skillet.

Made my way to London.
Saw a guy, big guy, guy with a briefcase.
Followed him down the alley,
put my blade into his gut
and as the blood shot
I became him
like momma used to say
the loaf became Jesus.

I am Elvis Presley.
I am Ted Hughes.

At my poetry readings I sneer and rock my hips.
I stride the moors
in a white satin jump suit,
bloated as the full moon.

Bless my soul,
what's wrong with me?

At night I sit in my room
and I write, and the great bulbous me
slaps a huge shadow on the wall.

I am writing a poem
about the death of the Queen Mother
but it won't come right.

I look up. Outside a fox peers at me.
I sing softly to it,
strumming my guitar.

Soon, all the foxes
and the jaguars and the pigs
and the crows are gathering
outside my window, peering in.

Ian McMillan

I sing Wooden Heart, Blue Hawaii.
There is the small applause
of paws and feathers.

I am Ted Hughes. I am Elvis Presley.
I am down at the end of lonely street
and a jump suit rots in a southern coffin
as people pay their respects to a barrage balloon.

I sit here,
I can feel the evening shrinking me
smaller and smaller.
I have almost gone. Ted,
three inches long, perfect.
Elvis, Ted.

TOM LEONARD

from: **Scenes from Scottish Literary Life**

(1)
o am no a
ehm
am noa ehm

puritan like
naw
nay wey

jist
ahm eh
am

that eh
serious
its

ma art
aye
fuck me am

aye

thats it

Tom Leonard

(2)

one of those writers always suspicious of laughter
at the heart of whose work is a concept of masculinity

sifting for sellouts every chuckle of an audience
mean hombres don't look for approval know what I mean

hung up on reverence for the cowboy
lolling home from the frontier, pioneer

swashbuckling shucks, washbucklin sucks
nickers off ready when I come home

(3)

Your work has been declared relevant
by the vanguardist literary publication
of a southern foreign capital.

Receive two invitations to launches:
but be warned -
Some of your friends are now enemies

(5)

the haemorrhoidal pot-bellied visiting dialect poet
silently eases a blood-drenched fart

into the already semiotically overladen immediate ambience
of the incessantly talking lecturer on socio-psycho-linguistics

(6)

the excited blurb

...larger than life,
it is smaller than the Cosmos only by
that volume which you now hold in your hand.
This book is all that it is not!

(7)

AFTER THE NUCLEAR OBLITERATION OF SCOTLAND, A FRAGMENT OF A
LONG POEM IS FOUND IN A LEAD COFFIN

Of course as Stalin clearly demonstrated in *Marxism and Problems of Linguistics:*

...the significance of the so-called gesture language, in view of its extreme poverty and
limitations, is negligible. Properly speaking, this is not a language, and not even a linguistic substitute that could in one way or another replace spoken language, but an aux-
iliary means of extremely limited possibilities to which man sometimes resorts to
emphasise this or that point in his speech. Gesture language and spoken language are
just as incomparable as are the primitive wooden hoe and the modern caterpillar tractor
with its five-furrow plough or tractor row drill.

Tom Leonard

This in incontrovertible contradistinction to the terracing rice-pudding-brain
whose idea of Scottish Literature consists of readings from Charlie Tully's *Passed
to You:*

If I had a pound for every time I've sent a corner kick swinging into the goalmouth at
practice, I'd be a millionaire. When I'm at outside-left, I place the ball in the arc, take a
step back and send it over with my right foot. I reverse the procedure if I'm on the right.
This is the only proper way to take a flag kick - that is, if you want to put the ball into
the danger zone. The ball takes a curve and swings in on goal making it awkward for a
goalkeeper to cover it all the way.

Slouch

Their barstools have slouched them too early
though later half-cut they start to sidle up

'Hey Pat, why not fuck off where you came,
back to the bogs, shouldn't you be pickin' spuds?'

They have eyes with no causes, their smug voices
in drunken unison jeer & mock my voice.

Perhaps when the hangover hits i'll take them up,
return meekly, submerge myself in landscape,

more like submerge myself in Black Bush -
bury myself in selfish small-town intrigue,

or if i had any passion left for bland slogans
i could even do my bit for the 'armed struggle'.

But the echo of Lambegs burst my skull,
i've spent too long licking up to England.

i've been the brunt of their stunted comedians
i've lived in comfort but amid canned laughter

& this latest encounter could come to fisticuffs
although til now i've played the Irish card with charm.

They probe me: 'Mick, do you even belong in this country?'
i won't slouch too early so i gleefully reply

'just as much as you belong in mine'...

PETER FINCH

Dribble Creeps

There are three skinheads in the furniture department
trying to shop-lift a bed.
It won't fit in the lift.
This is for the middle-class and full.
Already a member has fainted
confronted with swearing, tattooed sweat.
No one is sure anyway that these charmers
should not do what they do.
Only the floor manager,
cowering in the demonstration kitchen
knows what will happen next.

The trio traverse his terrain
trailing an upended slumberland
which bangs the lights
and cracks the fire-door architrave.
Trembling, he tries the phone
but gets no answer.
Security are chatting to friends,
the line is engaged.

On the escalator shoppers assume the lollards
to be larking employees. Their garb is in keeping.
There is no argument.
The posture springs bounce through perfumery.
This is a free country.

Two women wearing designer face cream
shake their heads .

Is not every juvenile delinquent the
evidence of a family in which the
family bond is weakened and loosened?
Is not every dishonest apprentice an
evidence of the same; every ruined
female; every ruined youth, the infinite
numbers of unruly and criminal people who
now swarm on the surface of this great
kingdom; and inundate the streets of
these great cities and double-park
their vehicles with lights flashing as
if this gave them permission. Are
not these hoards on bicycles who
never stop at red lights, these can kickers,
spitters, hooligan rampagers, skate boarders,
screamers, these riff-raff who
knock unasked on doors, pathetically
enquiring if you want your windows double-glazed.

Are not these the evidence we need?

The bed is left smashed and unslept in
at the end of the fruit market.
At night it is a target for junior Rimbauds
launching Astra skyrockets through drain-pipes.
When it catches fire the yobs piss on it.

The manager calls this shrinkage.
It is an accountancy term.

ell preperte es theft

ill priporti is thift

oll proporto os thoft

ull prupurtu us thuft

all praparta as tha

prip op prapap

prapap pop pop

preee

keep peep eep eep

prefot pre fat rop

rop rop

rop rop

rop rop

rop rop

rop

profit drive

drum drum

rum drum

drum drum

dribble creeps

Hills

Just an ordinary man of the bald Welsh hills,
docking sheep, penning a gap of cloud.
Just a bald man of the ordinary hills,
Welsh sheep gaps, docking pens, cloud shrouds.
Just a man, ordinary, Welsh doctor, pen weaver,
cloud gap, sheep sailor, hills.
Just a sharp shard, hill weaver, bald sheep,
pilot pen rider, gap doctor, cloud.
Just a shop, sheer hill weaver, slate,
balder, cock gap, pen and Welsh rider,
Just slate shop, hill balder, cocking,
shop gap. Welsh man, cloud pen.
Just shops, slate, cocks, bald sheep,
Welsh idea, gutteral hills, ordinary cloud.
Just grass gap, bald gap, garp grap,
grap shot sheep slate, gap grap.
garp gap
gop gap
sharp grap shop shap
sheeep sugar sha
shower shope sheep
shear shoe slap sap
grasp gap gosp gap
grip gap grasp gap
guest gap grat gap
gwint gap grog gap

growd gap gost gap

gap gap gwin gap

gap gop gwell gap

gap gop gap gap

gap gap gap gap

gap gap gorp gap

gap gap gap gap

gap gap gap gap

gap gap gap gap

gap gap gap gap

gap gap gap

immigrant slate mirth grot gap,

bald grass, rock gap, shot gap,

old Welsh shot gap, rumble easy,

old gold gap, non-essential waste gap,

rock docker, slow slate gap, empty rocker

rate payer, wast gap, cloud hater,

grasper balder, pay my money, dead,

trout shout, slate waste. language nobody

uses, bald sounds, sends, no one pens,

fire gap, failed gasps,

dock waste, holiday grey gap,

hounds, homes, plus fours, grip sheep,

four-wheeled Rover: Why Not? Soft price,

Grown gavel, sais.

The problem gaps, ordinary television,

nationalist garbage, insulting ignorance,

shot sheep, uninvited bald interference,
don't need real sheep where we are,
sheepless, sheepless, Welsh as you are, still,
no gasps, gogs or gaps for us,
no,
point our aerials at the Mendip Hills.

B_{OB} C_{OBBING}

FLAP	CLINK	TINK	THUMP	THUD	BUMP
POUND	PLUMP	PLOP	PLONK	PLUNK	CRUNK
SNAP	CRICK	CLACK	BOOM	GRATE	CLUNK
SLAM	BANG	FLIP	FLICK	JERK	YERK
JOG	JOLT	BUTT	TAP	RAP	DINT
CLUB	BIFF	BASH	BOX	SPAR	CROWN
SLOSH	SOCK	SLUG	COSH	THRASH	BEAT
CANE	FLOG	STRAP	DUST	TAN	TRESS
SQUASH	SWAT	FLAIL	MAUL	STONE	PELT
BAT	SWIPE	CRACK	CUT	SCUTCH	SCRATCH
KNOCK	DAB	PAT	NUDGE	DIG	CUFF
CLUMP	THWACK	THRUST	KICK	FLING	LUNGE
DRIVE	CLIP	GOAD	TAMP	PROD	DENT
PUNCH	SMASH	PRESS	TOSS	JIG	JAR
BOUNCE	ROCK	TWITCH	ITCH	THRILL	THROB
WRITHE	SQUIRM	FLOP	ROLL	REEL	PITCH
SWAG	WAG	LURCH	WHIRR	WHIRL	HOP
ROAR	CAP	PLUCK	FRET	FUME	FUSS
STAMP	STEW	GUST	STORM	WINCE	FLINCH
BLINK	SHRINK	CROUCH	START	FLUSH	SHOCK
STUN	WHIP	HIDE	CLOUT	JOUNCE	PULSE
SWAY	BOB	RAMP	RAGE	JIB	WHIFF
LID	TOP	PLUG	BUNG	SLAT	HOOD

YARR   YAUP   YARK   YOWL   YACK
YADDER   YAH   YAFF   YAFFLE
YELP   YAPP   YAHOO   YALE
YAMMER   YABBER   YAMPH   YARKEN
YARL   YARM   YAW   YAW-HAW
YAWL   YAWLER   YAWPER   YEET
YAW-YAW   YDAD   YED   YEDDER
YE-HO   YEI   YELL   YELLOGH
YEP   YERK   YERR   YEX   YEST
YHELLE   YIKE   YIP   YIRR
YO   YOAKS·   YODEL   YOICKS
YOKER   YOAK   YOLL   YOLP
YOMER   YOOP   YOLA   YOMMER
YOUDLE   YOWT   YUCKLE   YAK
YATTER   YOP   YUP   YAKALO

GERALDINE MONK

Departure (after Max Beckman)

craving for fruits
cool
skin dewelled sanctity to
caress
to press on
    lips cheeks
- at least remembrance of -
pear grapes apples

    fish
    NO
WE DIDN'T REHEARSE IT LIKE THIS
stumped turquoise
      aztecing sun-lust
      fertility bled to
      futility
      rites
    corrupt with torture

King-fisher
    blue crowning
    gold horizons

Queening peace and sea
    with warm

Child like
  we are

sailing new and speechless
    soon
re-making   language
with guards even
out the picture

The murder everyone commits
stepwiz   leather-lean
no relieving sigh songster
no surrender no
hole to crawl in
side out side up
tight outa sight
da da
    candle light no
brighter than fish skins blind
folding on blind
lemon scared and sickly
drumming up to death as
broken   as broken
followthoughts through
trying   to
remember   the future

AARON WILLIAMSON

from: A Holythroat Symposium

Malo is taking part in a book. In order to do so, he endeavours at re-membering the anatomy and physiology of speech, as if, in some way, he could enchant those for whom the book waits. Soon, it is apparent that each organ concerned with speech production, is so only secondarily to some other, more urgent function - respiration, swallowing, lubricance. Eating and chewing food. Malo decides to place these first, too. Now, when struggling at the console of the switchboard he contrived, (to mediate the surges and absences within the book), all he hears at first is the heaving of diaphragm, swilling sluices, moans and bolts.

The solution is direct. Malo is extirpating the vocal tract with knives. In sleep: the stealth of his hand as it slides through his mouth, down, past the snarlings of his larynx to the cavernous holes of the burning thorax. The blade, tiny and swift betwixt efferent fingers, flickers at the neural raiment. Malo, swallowing his arm, chews it down into his stomach. Malo: an ouroboros circling in the night. At work: filleting the noisome kit.

And in the morning, severed from its mortal casing, the bladderlung hangs loose inside, punctured and sucked out of breath. When the sun draws its legion it is to spit itself, inverted, into the air with a last momentous spasm.

The voice is to be rebuilt. To voice: a verb. To utter, somehow, in words. Now, everything speaks; and yet, is one voice. Malo moves in its signal box, muttering with activity. The walls, curious with lettering, fluctuate precisely to the workings of its heart. Without oral features, parts of the book arrive. Malo becomes hand signals. Leg kicks. A rib begins to knit itself, illegibly, around adjacent ribs. We are wiring in. Drunk with intrusions. Squalls of supersaturating sonic; a cacklebabble shunting through its haywire sermoning, scouring for its screed. This is the lodestar. Its Holythroat. Convening at the neck with host imbibers. Randomly. A Holythroat Symposium.

AARON WILLIAMSON

from: Freedom, Liberty & Tinsel

Existence has no exit
bulbed up on fuckout,
snapped out of exits
evil out of I-head:
what am I even doing here?
- I found out at last;
I was an ex-it,
simply a do-nut torn out of the sky
through which the coming dawn
commuters form
convulsions of birds
goin'
think I'd scorch my wings?

- well I could die
just for opening my mouth
I mean speaking such shit
I mean to be killed
by Satan and
HIS sidekick
- I'm no buddah,
I'm a wanker:
Buddah can you spare me a dimension?
How clever. Wanker.
Or just a mention?
- upon the smooth floors of galaxies...

You see?
I have with me, at all times,
the magic words
with which to form a sentence
of death.
Of course, I can't SAY them,
they're not playthings
...I grew a flower that filled me
with tears;
feathers upon my teeth,
my nerves were sticking out HERE
far enough to form wings:
a pair of clipped and soiled
wings
that flap but never get me
in the air:

I do nothing,
I go nowhere,
I see no-one.

think I'd scorch my wings?

KEITH JAFRATE

Acappella

1

to pay for pleasure with good work
craft of the touch that opens roses
music made from the fall of iron
music made from the scale rain plays
falling through an iron bridge
music lost in the swirl of barley

music calling from a woman's laughter
calling calling to be pure and flying
loose from the beautiful cage of dying

music without reason like death
music without measurement like death
music risen from ten thousand lives
that *holds* that life
voice without mouth
dance without ankles
kiss

kiss

2

you've seen the worst
that I can do

Africa do not desert me Africa
never leave me in the dark
without your blue wisdom
Africa I want your children

you've seen my father change
like a knife turned in a white
light in my blue eyes Africa
do not leave me in this European winter

I bring the tongue of a soft spring
these animals of grass
waking Africa
waking to the work of rain
never leave me white
alone here without dreaming

you've seen my heart's glass mouth bite
smiled for me when I was bone
do not desert me Africa
I want your children

3

making a flower of themselves
where his lover's face sleeps
making one caress a curve
a bird's parabola
over her golden surface

Carlos tells me how
his hands can't
flatten that image but must play
turning like leaves continuously
over
Carlos tells me how his hands can't
hold straight lines
whereas water

water runs to them
threaded with sunlight
he pours his hands out for us
over us laughing

4

when he flies like a bird
he is not that bird
he walks on glass in this world
breathes in water

when he falls like a stone
he is not that stone
but the song a stone holds
yearning

I would tell you all I know of him
but he hides like a bird and is not that bird
he flies like a bird and does not fly

where dumb things call him
mouths wise with hurting

he bathes in screaming
screams he stole from headless lovers
screams he stole from faceless kisses
kisses trapped in a world of suckers
where he speaks

his words are weights of ice
he soars like a bird and is not that bird

NEIL SPARKES

everything

the story's in the rock
stories in the stone
pulled from the earth
from under you

there were times
i was always on the move
never in one place
never ever standing still

you're a love of mine
i'll treat you fine
never pull the rug
from under you

there's more things
under the sun
there's everything
there's everything for you

manchild and hunter
travelling on a journey
the end not always in sight

trusting in luck
trusting in love

always trying
to live and learn

under a canopy of blue
just take the time
to look around
and you will find

there's more things
under the sun
there's everything
there's everything for you

the rains fall
but how can i tell
how much i feel
i'm scared of being wrong

you're a love of mine
i watch your eyes
your smile lives here
even when you're gone

our love is in the earth
we can watch it
spread and grow
watch it spread and grow

walkabout

i believe in the devil
and the spirits in the trees

i believe when the storm blows
the wind talks to me

i believe in the cool tides
and sweet serendipity

i believe in love
and that time will tell

well i believe i might've known you
when you were somebody else

i believe there's a reason
why we get on so well

walkabout boy, walkabout boy
just take a stroll through the trees

i believe i'll send a raven
to steal your soul

believe there's so much to learn
'til the day we grow old

there's more in this world
than we'll ever know, i believe

walkabout boy, walkabout boy,
just take a stroll through the trees

well i'm leaving town
when the moon's full tonight

tired of trains and stations
i want to change the way i live my life

i believe i'd take you with me
if you'd like

i need someone like you
in my life

everyday's another heartache
everyday so much more in love with you

i'm a walkabout boy
and i'm enjoying the view

i need someone like you
in my life.

LEVI TAFARI

A Picture

I wonna paint a picture
a heartical picture
one that's BLACK and WHITE
Got to paint this picture
relative to matter
to instruct too delight
Can you see this picture
revealing I culture
documenting time
I could use a camera
with instant colour
but that's not my style.

I kinda get the feeling
If I paint this picture
things will start to change
If I paint this picture
all in one colour
would you think I'm strange
It is an expression
which could be a lesson
one of love and hate
just let me paint this picture
in I own fashion
to communicate.

A thousand words could paint a picture
I need to create
Words or colours I don't partial
no need for a debate
Shapes form images in this picture
unfolding mysteries
Well this might SHOCK you
even rock you
don't put it inna gallery.

I didn't paint this picture
to confuse you
or confuse myself
you're living under an illusion
if you think this picture
will bring me wealth
You see I could be prophet
but me I'm just a poet
I don't want a prize
Yes I will use WORDS
to paint this one
cause it's a POEM in disguise.

LEVI TAFARI

Blues Dance Sufferers Style

Beating, bouncing, bubbling,
reggae music jumps out
from a dread sound system
riding on clouds of smoke
vibrating through the structure
of the building
communicating to the people
bring forth a message of redemption
Bob Marley sings a song
with a Rasta connection.
Brothers and sisters rocking
entwined like a root
that keeps on growing.
Blues dance sufferers style
the DJ play
and the DJ say
"Guh deh cause yuh,
wicked and wild
Roots rock don't stop
Yuh haffe move forward".

Darkness fills the room
Ites, gold and green
shines brightly
Beaming like the full moon
the vibes a run right

the atmosphere gets bubbly.
Cans of red stripe flowing
like a never ending stream
that keeps on running.
The partaking of the peace pipe
the smell of the herb is ire
mixed with curry goat and rice
the kitchen plays its part
and the dance smell nice.
Blues dance sufferers style
the DJ play
and the DJ say
"Guh deh cause yuh
wicked and wild,
Roots rock don't stop
Yuh haffe move forward".

A commercial break
it's a soul earthquake
some get funky.
Soul heads bop to the music
slipping and sliding
they would never refuse it
Lovers dance cheek to cheek
while skankers skank the late hour
dripping in sweat
like them just get a shower
hold tight, each night

this is Black music.
Battling two sound systems
competition takes place in the blues dance
DJ flashing lyrics rapidly
get flat or get shot
keep moving.
Ravers coming and going
checking out the various sessions
nuff dance inna de area
which one should yuh check
it's a dread decision.
Blues dance sufferers style
the DJ play
and the DJ say
"Guh deh cause yuh
wicked and wild
Roots rock don't stop
Yuh haffe move forward".

All shades of people inna de blues dance
dubbing to the sounds of dub
sanctuary inna de ghetto
an escape from the commercial club.
Discos are too clinical
the DJ's in control
disco lights imposing
to the sound of rock and roll,
the music shuts down early

just as you get hyped
the night is young
and yuh want fe rave
that style is not your type.
Yuh reach the blues dance late
yuh pay the musical rate
and yuh forward through the gate
fe guh listen to dub plate
sweet reggae music.
Blues dance sufferers style
the DJ play
and the DJ say
"Guh deh cause yuh
wicked and wild
Roots rock don't stop
Yuh haffe move forward
move forward
move forward
inna Blues dance".

Benjamin Zephaniah

A Writer Rants

Write a rant about de runnings
Writer rant about de runnings
So I wrote of fires burning
An de judgement dat is coming.
It is part of our tradition
It's our fighters ammunition,
Give it schools fe education
It may start some love creation.

So I did it, yes I wrote it
Den I went around an spoke it.
It has come from off de bookshelf
It's alive so hear it yourself,
A spirit came to me and said
"You have a job you must do, dread,
Write a rant of our short-comings"
Writer rant about de runnings!

A Modern Slave Song

When you're cosy in your house
Remember I exist,
When you drink expensive drink
Remember I exist,
When you're lying on my beach

Remember I exist,
When you're trying to sell my beans to me
Remember I exist.

When you're loving each other to death
Remember I exist,
When you're selling me my music
Remember I exist,
When you sell dat cotton shirt
Remember I exist,
When you're interviewing me
Remember I exist.

I was the first inventor - remember
I am black and dread and love - remember
I am poor but rich, don't mess - remember
I am history - remember.
You tried to shut my mouth - remember
You studied me and filmed me - remember
You're spending my money - remember
You're trying to forget me but remember.

Remember I am trained to not give in,
So don't forget,
Remember I have studied studying
So don't forget.
Remember where I come from, cause I do.
I won't forget.

Remember you got me, cause I'll get you.
I'll make you sweat.

Big Boys Rich

Big Boy Richy wants to mek a profit,
Sue wants a kidney,
Tony wants a job,
Errol wants freedom,
Tom wants clean air to breathe.
Big Boy Richy wants to buy a rocket,
Jenny and Paul want a zebra-crossing,
Ms. Campbell de teacher wants recognition,
Old-timer Larry wants a pension
And Sgt. Mollins wants a conviction.
Big Boy Richy wants old champagne,
Dis child needs fresh water,
Danny needs a pair of shoes,
Mom needs a fifty pence piece for de meter,
And dis guy said if him don't get some kinda
Voice in parliament him will blow de place
Up, and watch it fall down.

Big Boy Richy wants a war.
Him sey him wants to protect Sue, Tony, Errol, Tom,
Jenny, Paul, Ms. Campbell, Larry, Sgt. Mollins, dis child,
Danny and Mom and many other guys including you and me.

Big Boy Richy says he never got where he
Is today by sitting pon him backside
Complaining about the state of de world.

John Hegley

Overruling The Bank Of England

The Queen wears glasses
But not on any of them banknotes.
She wears many a gem
but not the sparkling jewels
of her glasses
and there must be some occasions
when she's wondering where they've
gone
but we can help the Queen
by taking pen to paper
and carefully putting them on.

Glasses Good Contact Lenses Bad

In the embrace of my glasses
I openly accept my vulnerability
and affirm my acceptance of outside help.
As well as providing the open acknowledgement
of the imperfection of my eyesight
my glasses are a symbolic celebration
of the wider imperfection that is the human condition.
In contrast contact lenses are a hiding of the fault.
They pretend the self-sufficiency of the individual
and minister unto the cult of stultifying normality,
they are that which should be cast out of your vision:

they are a denial of the self,
they are a denial of the other,
they are a betrayal of humanity.

The Briefcase

from the very beginning I loved my glasses
the eye test made me feel important
I wanted to be colour blind as well
for some reason I was never teased about them as a child
not even at the grammar school
where daily they would mock my briefcase
because it was not made of leather
as I recall there was only ever one boyhood jibe
aimed at my glasses
and this a fairly oblique one
oi double glazing
where did you get that plastic briefcase?
in adult years I got a lot more trouble
on one occasion
a rabble
threw rubble
at my glasses
it was after this that I decided to take action
I bought myself a leather briefcase
and the next day set out to face my building site tormentors
somehow the briefcase in my hand
was a stand

against a land
which had gradually lost its magic for me
a joyful absurdity
in the face
of the tragically commonplace
as I approached the contractors
for once it felt like MY world again
what have you got in the briefcase then four eyes?
was the question
POWER was the reply
the power of the human imagination
and I walked proudly
and steadily past them
in a shower of flying masonry

MARSHA PRESCOD

Big Time

One day, my poem upped and said to me,
"Look kid, sorry to say this,
But whilst our relationship was meaningful,
It's time we chose our different paths"
"But I gave birth to you!" I wailed,
Whilst it threw a Dorothy Parker leer,
Swept out to see its analyst,
Leaving me to weep into my thesaurus.

From then on,
It was all downhill for me,
Only puns and epigrams
Shared my lonely life,
An affair with a passing sonnet
Came to nothing.

As years went by,
I glimpsed my former rhyme,
On the cover of Time and Vogue,
Meeting with Popes and Presidents,
Profiled in the Sundays.

I saw my poem one last time
On the horizon,
Cruising in Gucci shades,
Talking out of the side of its mouth,

Doing deals with agents.
Tanned (from a skiing weekend with Jackie O)
It was smiling, deeply insincere,
Sitting, giving autographs to Mick,
And fixing up an interview on the Late Show.

And in sodden (but literate) misery
I yelled,
"You're nothing but a jumped up limerick!
I knew you when you were only a piece of graffitti....."
The last words I ever spoke,
For my poem sent
Heavies, in mohair Brook Bros suits
To work me over
With copies of
Its Channel 4 contract.

JOOLZ

No Place Like Home

It's like water dripping on a stone, really, the water torture; drip, drip, dead slow but horribly unending, they never let up. The minute she got in today they started on her, about the company she keeps this time, surprise, surprise...22 and still at home. Man, she thinks, it's no joke but it's funny, ha ha ha.

Patty lights another cigarette from the stub of the last one and notices without much surprise that her hand is shaking. The tape player auto reverses for the second time and she can't be bothered to change the music. She knows, not just assumes - but knows, that her Mother is making that pinched, furious expression because the rumbling noise of the band can be heard downstairs, if not in the street. She ought to turn it down but she doesn't, so she feels guilty, but she always feels guilty about something or other so she lets it play; childish, she admits that, but so what, she's got no other vices - no lovers, she's not a druggie or a drinker, she pays her whack from what little she earns at the shop...oh, what does it matter. She begins to mimic her Mother's voice talking to her Father, who without doubt is taking refuge behind the evening paper.

"Listen to that, Michael, listen, the noise is dreadful, why we haven't had complaints yet I don't know. What is she doing up there all the time anyhow? It's not normal...Michael, you're not listening to me. I'm very worried, it could be drugs or anything...oh, we never had this trouble with Mark..."

Drip, drip, drip. Patty begins to laugh silently, the horrible panic feeling swelling in her like a huge balloon, she feels sick and screamy, she wants to run downstairs and shout:

"Mark? Mark? What do you know about bloody Mark? He may be your precious fuck-ing golden boy, but he's smashed out of his brain every night and he's a complete bastard, a real bastard. Why don't you ask Sara Chatham why she had to have the abortion, Mother, and who boasted about 'getting away with it' in the pub?...but he can do no wrong, can he Mother, because he went to university, played the game like he always did to your faces, and I stayed here..."

Drip, drip, drip. Jeez, Patty could see her Mother's face now, and hear the grinding litany of complaints that would fall out of her parents' mouths - letting down the family, disgraceful behaviour, what will people think, swearing, and as for your clothes...oh, Mam, Mam, isn't there anything left for me? I love you. I love me Dad. I want to love you, but you don't give me anything to hold onto. You're sealed up together like an iceberg...do you worship Mark because he left, 'treat 'em mean, keep 'em keen', is that it? I can't do it. If you're disappointed in me, Mam, then god knows I'm fucked up because of you, and it's not my fault. It's not. Oh, the world is closing round me like a trap...animals chew their own legs off to escape the snare, don't they?

The music smashes round the little room like an anaesthetic, numbing her while she cries, heaving and retching, hugging herself into a tight ball...She'll leave soon, she knows it. But she'll never have what she craves so much, she'll go not with a proud send off, the college scarf and a blind sense of a favourite's selfish power, but furiously, and far too late, hanging on until the last minute, trying to batter down the glassy wall of her parents' inability to comprehend her passion, hating them for being wrong and hating herself for her fury.

Poor child, there are other ways to hurt than with the fist or the stick, and the ones that leave no mark still leave scars just as ugly. You can love them, your Mam and Dad, but you don't have to like them, and it's when you can forgive them for their failure and their selfishness, for only being human, that you can make some life for yourself...

Kings of the World

Barry jerks awake in the reddish gloom of the living room, his legs agonisingly stitched with cramp. For a few blank seconds he can't remember where he is, he had been entangled in a dream where his mother had been calling him for school with the insane repetition of a jackhammer. He rolls off the dusty sofa still wrapped in his doss bag and futiley tries to massage his calves. Eventually the twisting pain subsides and he staggers, unbalanced, into the kitchen and taking a mug out of the pile of unwashed pots, he spoons some instant coffee into it and fills it up from the hot tap...he gropes for his fags and lights up taking a savage lungful and rubbing his rough chin...where the fuck am I he thinks, eyeing the greasy room...oh yeah, this must be Mandy's gaff, course, we come here after the party...jesus my head kills...that gear must have been dog fucking rough...

Upstairs, Mandy shifts about uncomfortably in the sour tangle of nylon quilts, Richie snoring into her right ear. She wishes the baby would just be born and get it over with, it's doing her head in dragging this lump about, thank christ Jane gave her that huge baggy all in one, at least she doesn't have to look totally stupid...she reaches out from the mattress with a greenish white arm and fumbles about on the floor for the half smoked joint she left there last night. Lighting it, she draws deep and shakes Richie awake. "Go and make some tea, Rich, go on..." "Gimme some of that first, cowbag," he grunts and taking the glowing stub he stumbles downstairs in his raggy old trackie bottoms...

There's no point drawing the curtains, so they just sit in the half dark and watch T.V. while they do a few hot knives. Then, while Mandy goes and paints her face, the boys do a bit of whizz and share a can of lager. When Mandy appears in her purple baggy and ethnic type skull cap, her lips as red as the broken gas fire's glow, they get a taxi into town and hit the pub where they've arranged to score some E before going on to the rave...

Days pass like this,
Weeks suck past in a fever.
Barry stays with Mandy and Rich for a couple of months, then wanders off to the Midlands because it's a happening sort of place at the moment and he doesn't want to stick around after the birth, the thought of the baby and the attendant hassle unnerves him.

Behind the fragile shelter of their imitation pride, that swaggers and brags of outlaw romance and a fine contempt for the world and its realities, the children sit; knees pulled up and hands clamped tight over their ears, their eyes and mouths sealed shut. They rock back and forth silently...soft and weak, unable to deal with their own flawed and human selves.

Mandy's baby is stillborn. Rich goes back to his mum for the fourth time and Barry gets arrested and sent down for running someone else's coke.

Dream on. It'll be over soon enough.

Fintra

The beach is flat from the retreating tide
scoured and icy in the bitter winds.
The tangle of stones, sea darkened driftwood
and the scummy litter of humanity
catches at my feet and trips me
as I walk towards the water...

...Blown spray whips me,
I can taste salt...I can taste salt...I will not cry.
Overhead, gulls screech against the brewing gale
and the dull emerald of the breakers
meets the strand in explosions over and over.
My hands are so cold...
The last time we were here
you held my hands and rubbed them warm,
I can taste salt...I can taste salt...I will not cry.

...Breathing in the corrosive air
burns my lungs, and the sand sucks at my boots
as I tread unsteadily.
I love this place, bound by mountains,
their cliffs plunging into the white foam,
the long falls of stone patched with cushiony spreads of green,
the light rolling in vivid chases over the land and sea
like a child's kaleidoscope.
It hardly seems real, but as I put my face up to the cloud whitened sun

JOOLZ

I can taste salt...I can taste salt...I will not cry...
because if I do, I will not stop, I could not stop,
and all the oceans wouldn't be as salt as those tears...

If you are no longer here
at least you are in the world,
and the light that shines bloody through my closed eyelids
somewhere shines on you...
Oh, I can taste salt...but I will not cry,
Not in this day, or the long night coming...

The Prize

Don't box me in, I said
I'm not your prize for
years of self-denial
your sacrifice was not for me
you don't care who I want to be
there for use I became your excuse
to stay in a loveless marriage
put up with a barrage of
insult and abuse
while the lid pressed down to
obscure the light of my own reality

Afraid to live, afraid to die
you sit there stuck and wonder why
I moved away, made a life that
makes no sense to you
make love with the 'wrong' people
why I make you feel so uncomfortable

You cannot tape my mouth with guilt
plug the holes with religious crap
or tie me to your status trap
I burn your letters, stay away
won't play your games of gross denial
I was not a happy child

MÁIGHRÉAD MEDBH

Easter 1991

I am Ireland
and I'm sick,
sick in the womb,
sick in the head,
and I'm sick of lying
in this sick-bed,
and if the medical men
don't stop operating
I'll die.

I am Ireland
and if I die,
my name will go down
in the censor's fire.
My face in the mirror is shy.
I have painted it too many times.
There's nothing to like
about this kind of beauty.

I am Ireland
and I don't know what I am.
They tell me things in sham films
like The Field, that the travellers
are pink-faced romantics in fairy caravans,
that my villages are full of
eejits and ludramáns,

that my pagan power is dead.
It was made for Hollywood,
not me.

I am Ireland
and I'm silenced.
I cannot tell
my abortions, my divorces,
my years of slavery,
my fights for freedom.
It's got to the stage
I can hardly remember
what I had to tell,
and when I do,
I speak in whispers.

I am Ireland
and I have nowhere to run.
I have spent my history
     my energy
     my power
     my money
to build him up
and he gave me back
nothing I didn't take myself.

Inside my head, the facts are loud.
Only two women's shelters in Dublin.

MÁIGHRÉAD MEDBH

On Stephen's Day,
a man petrol-bombs one
and on the same day
gets out on bail.
Abortion is a criminal offence.
Abortion information is stopped.
Divorce is denied.
The guards don't interfere.
The facts are loud.
Sharon Gregg dies in Mountjoy.
Patrick Sheehy dies in Nenagh.
Fergal Carraher dies in Cullyhanna.
Men get life terms for self-defence.
Dessie Ellis is handed on a stretcher to my enemy.
The facts are loud.
Bishop Cathal Daly
wants less talk of AIDS.
Thousands emigrate each year.
Half of my children are poor
and the poorest of all
are my daughters.

I am Ireland
and the poor die young
and the poor are easily sold
and the poor are the ones who fight
and because they fight, they die.

I am Ireland
and the Angelus Bell is tolling for me.
This illegal border will always be
unless we get up off our bended knee.
The priests run my schools and my history.
There's no free state
in the Catholic see.

I am Ireland
and I'm sick,
sick of this tidy house
where I live,
that reminds me of nothing,
not of the past,
not of the future.
I'm sick of depression
I'm sick of shame
I'm sick of poverty
I'm sick of politeness
I'm sick of looking over my shoulder
I'm sick of standing by the shore
waiting for some prince
to come on the tide.

Mise Éire
agus an ghaoth ag eirí láidir i mo chluasa
agus n'fheadar an é biseach nó bás a thiocfaidh.

MÁIGHRÉAD MEDBH

Mise Éire
agus n'fheadar an bhfuil mé óg nó sean.

Mise Éire
agus níl mé ag feitheamh a thuilleadh.

I am Ireland
and I'm not waiting anymore.

Maybe It Was 1970

Kids running petrol bombs,
barricades and binlids,
cars blazing,
overturned on telly.

Bernadette Devlin shouting.
She was a student and
she was a MP.
She was a cheeky wee monkey.

On the news Dad's shop burning down.
My mascara had run.

Maybe it was 1970.
The reverend Ian Paisley
crushed through a window
on the telly.
His hand bled.
'For God's sake, this is madness. Go home.'
How could a minister be bad?
Blood ran freely down his wrist
like roads,
like the red hand of Ulster
    severed.

CHERRY SMYTH

Maybe it was 1977.
On the news Dad's shop burning down.
I was at Kelly's.
It came on in the bar.
I was in love with Shawn Logan.
I didn't know whether to kiss or cry.
I wanted him. I wanted to go home.
He was much older.
He was a Catholic.
He held me in his car.
It was a BMW.
He tried to touch me.
'Don't,' I said. 'I've got a tampax in.'
But I wanted him.
His words were pure love,
'I don't mind,' he said.
My mascara had run.
I should have gone home.

Not everything was destroyed.
That was worse.
They sold the damage.
Salvaging charred dresses, odd shoes,
scalded mannequins.
Everything rained on.
Shawn chewed chewing gum.
So did I.

I looked at faces differently.
Daddy was quiet for a long time.

A Mother's Story

I could write a story,
my mother said,
you know, for one of those magazines
that gives prizes for true stories.
I could say how I've survived
my epileptic son,
my husband's nervous breakdown,
or a lesbian daughter.

Why can't you do something normal,
my mother asked,
like write a book
on vegetarian cookery,
that I could show my friends?
And why haven't you worked it out of your system yet?

Welcome home, she said,
(who's she, the cat's mother?)
You have Tom's room
and your nice wee friend
can sleep in here.
The spare room's been cleaned
for guests.

THE RIDGE COLLEGE LIBRARY

CHERRY SMYTH

It's all very well,
my mother said,
doing those things in England,
so long as you don't do them here.
The ill-feeling runs too deep.

My mother's story.
I try to laugh it off.
Like spit, it sticks.

Black Leather Jacket

My black leather jacket rubs and sticks,
hot and stubborn.
'You have to suffer for style.'
Your voice is wicked,
body like a stick insect,
in pyjamas with stripes,
saying 'hospital property'.

I hold your hand which is enormous
and want to fill the bed
with petals, silks, feathers to soften
the bones that tug at your skin
to run away.

The beard isn't you.

You don't smoke unfiltered Gauloises anymore.
The smell would rise from the garden
as you bent and planted and built
and trimmed and picked and
made so much from nothing.

Yesterday I bought flowers for you.
Marched them from Hyde Park to Trafalgar.
Wilting, rather ghastly dahlias
were all they had.
We were three thousand,
one for each who has died.
Men sobbed in Piccadilly
over white lilies,
hands tight on stems,
teeth sore.

You ask imperiously,
'Which is better, to be happy or to be right?'
I smile.
You would have scoffed at Louise Hay six months ago.
You look happy.
And haven't the wind to laugh.

'Go quickly now,' you order.
Your mouth moves like a butterfly under the mask.
'Take those yellow roses, all of them,
I've not enough room.'

CHERRY SMYTH

Your eyes are as big as your heart,
bluer than the sky you can't see from the bed.

Your black leather jacket creaks as I kiss you.
It rubs and sticks, smells of sex and clubs and streets
and tells of firm hands that have stroked it,
rushed it off, to love you.
It is important to keep it on.

Commitments

I will always be there.
When the silence is exhumed.
When the photographs are examined
I will be pictured smiling
among siblings, parents,
nieces and nephews.

In the background of the photographs
the hazy smoke of barbecue,
a checkered red-and-white tablecloth
laden with blackened chicken,
glistening ribs, paper plates,
bottles of beer, and pop.

In the photos
the smallest children
are held by their parents.
My arms are empty, or around
the shoulders of unsuspecting aunts
expecting to throw rice at me someday.

Or picture tinsel, candles,
ornamented, imitation trees,
or another table, this one
set for Thanksgiving,
a turkey steaming the lens.

My arms are empty
in those photos, too,
so empty they would break
around a lover.

I am always there
for critical emergencies,
graduations,
the middle of the night.

I am the invisible son.
In the family photos
nothing appears out of character.
I smile as I serve my duty.

Skin Catch Fire
for Dennis

In the very old sorrow of London,
beneath gull scarred skies
as raped cultures rise
to accuse and curse the crown,
in the drear light
sorrow casts over decay,
I leave you, in the care
of ancient snakes with ears.
I leave you in the lonely graffiti of:
'Smack keeps us warm

and we are loved'.

What will keep us warm?
A tender, burning nipple?
A gentle contusion on the neck
where we bit too hard
or sucked too long?
Will it be this memory
which guides our hands
along our thighs
to the rod of questions?

I leave you the power of hope
for a sane salvation.
Use it like bread,
trust it like a vow.
Beneath gull scarred skies
I leave. My laughter, a falcon
climbing above misery,
concealed in air.
It reaches your ears
as your name
touches my lips
causing my skin
to catch fire
like a city,
a phoenix,
a pyromantic.

N<small>EIL</small> B<small>ARTLETT</small>

That's What Friends Are For

My father said to me, he said, son, don't you ever worry about growing old?

He said, don't **you** ever worry about growing old?

And I said, well father what really worries me is whether I'll get the chance to grow old, I mean sometimes I wonder whether they're going to let us.......

But if I do, if I do grow old, then it's going to be just fine, it's going to be just fine, because I've got so many friends.

I've got so many friends.

I've got one to love me,
One to make love to me,
I've got one to lend me clothes, I've got one to take me dancing,
I've got four to keep me warm at night,
I've got seven to pick me up when I'm down,
I've got seven to pick me up anyway,
I've got -

He said, but don't you ever get scared?

I said well when I get scared then I just call up one of my friends.
He said, won't you be lonely?
I said, when I get lonely, I just call up my friends.
He said, but who's going to cook your dinner?

I said I'll cook the dinner, I'll invite some friends round;
and you can bring the wine.

He said, who's going to take you to the hospital.
I said, well, I'll just call up one of my friends.
He said;
You don't have a wife, you won't have any children, you don't even drive a car -
And I said it's going to be alright.
It is going to be alright,
Because I've got so many friends..............

And I called up my first friend and he said I'll be right over and I opened the door and he held out his hand and he took me in his arms and he held me tight and he held on to me, he held me together, he held me down, he laid me down and he made love to me all....night....long.

And I called up my second friend and he said, hello?, and I said, I'm sorry. I really don't know why I'm calling you, it's three o'clock in the morning, and he said, it's OK I was up anyway, I said yes but I don't know why I'm calling you, he said; it's okay, I can't sleep either, I don't know anyone who can these days.

And then I called up my third friend well he's not a friend really I just met him down the pub, it's the same every weekend I say don't do this to yourself, don't do it, but you know, what can you do, there you are, three o'clock in the morning and you're walking home together of course we couldn't get a taxi, three o'clock, there she is, walking down the middle of the bloody road, singing her head off, and I said, what is she like?

She's like a child, she's like my sister; she's like a mother to me that one, she's my best girl friend.

And I called up my fourth friend but he wasn't there so I called up my fifth friend and I said I'm so sad, he said it would be better to be angry, and I said I'm so sad, he said it would be better to be angry, I said; but I'm so sad. He said, you might feel better if you practised getting angry.

I called up my sixth friend and he said look I've got no more advice to give you but I can give you this if you think it will make you feel better and he gave me a big bottle of red wine and on the label he had written I KNOW JUST HOW YOU FEEL and that's what you need sometimes, someone who knows just exactly what it feels like..........

So I called up my seventh friend
And my seventh friend lent me his books, he lent me his records, he cooked me dinner, he drove me home and he put me to bed, he listened to my story, he heard me out, he talked me out of it, he disagreed with me;
He knew what he was saying;
He knew what he was talking about;
He made five practical suggestions about how I might improve my situation

My eighth friend checks me for bruises, he calls me back to make sure I'm alright and he lets me cry for as long as I want to and when we're walking down the street he never lets go of my hand, not ever.

And my ninth friend said do you know, I haven't had this much fun in three years........

and my tenth friend said Darling, I think I'm going to like you with white hair.......

and my Father said, but who's going to come to your funeral

.....................................and I said

..................................well I said
..................................That's What Friends Are For.

BELINDA BURTON

Alice in Acidland

Crystal Alice saw a man
With an axe last night;
She says hello to the
Postbox; Crystal Alice
Is a record with seven
Different tracks.

Crystal Alice is a
Chattering schoolgirl;
Crystal Alice is a
Born-again christian;
Alice is a thief,
She's a generous,
Warm-hearted young
Woman; She's a hippy,
She's a victorian
Lady; Crystal Alice
Is a psychoanalyst,
She wants to put you
In her pocket.

Crystal Alice has
Glittery spray in
Her hair; she has
Beads, she wears
Floaty skirts;

Crystal Alice has
A silver purse.

Crystal Alice hears
Whispering spirits;
Crystal Alice is
A floating soul.
She's tried to
Pin herself
To the ground
But Crystal Alice
Can't come down.

Horror in Toytown

We are the Toytown
People, and we pretend
To love each other,
We're the figment
Of some diseased
Inventor's warped
Imagination, we're
The victims of a
Genetic mutation,
We eat babies
And strangle grannies,
We're the weer queers.

We're the simulated people,
We're made of
Old tyres and rusty iron
And stuck together with
Fish eyes, we're the
Nasty people, we come out
And molest children
At night,
We haunt graves,
We never die,
We carry on,
We can't be strangled,
Gassed or hung,
We're immortal and morbid
Creatures, some of us
Disguised as teachers,
Mothers, judges and
Youth group leaders.

We're like a weed
Spreading everywhere,
We infest young minds
With our sordid lies,
We've killed the
Age of innocence
With our
Explicit literature;
We pretend to
Love each other,
We're the weer queers.

The Mary Whitehouse Nursery Rhyme

Eins, zwei, drei, vier,
You're a lessie, you're a queer,
If I had my way you wouldn't be here,
You've all got AIDS and you smell,
                    you smell.

Eins, zwei, drei,
You're a dirty spy,
You've come to spread corruption
And break family ties and you smell,
                    you smell.

Eins, zwei,
You're all spotty and why? Because
You've all got diseases and God's
Not on your side and you smell,
                    you smell.

Eins
I hate your faces,
All the bits are in the wrong places
And you're only bent 'cos you're ugly
You're a load of ugly-buglies and you smell,
                    you smell.

O-U-T spells OUT.

PATIENCE AGBABI

Serious Pepper

I.   Everyone's born
     no-one's found
     untill they find themselves

     hurting in the back of the throat
     because they've swallowed
     serious pepper   painful as truth.

     I used to eat cold meals all the time.
     They had been hot
     once.

     They held my nose and force
     fed me on two cultures
     egg and chips or eba and groundnut stew

     nothing got past the
     lump
     in my throat.

     In Sussex they used to say
     'You don't pronounce it like that
     in England. Did you pick it up from your

     parents?' In London
     'Your cockney voice is so ugly

Why can't you speak properly?'
And so often, 'You're so English.
I want to drive the English
ness out of you. Yes,

Too Black   Too White
in limbo   on the edge
of the dance floor. Playing gooseberry

but not found under a gooseberry bush.
I knew who my parents were
they natured and they nurtured me.

You can never forget that they love you
it spite of it all. In the 70's
I stopped playing

with dolls and began with words.
Red words   green words   yellow words
if I rubbed my eyes they stung me.

I was desperate
        disparate
        diasporate

Someone said recently
'It's always good to remember details
from the past'

but I'm always afraid
of serious pepper
painful as truth.

II. D'you know, I used to stick my fingers down
my throat so I didn't have to grow up
and find myself

but in spite of that my bust remained.
It stopped growing at the age of 12
but it grew heavier.

 The Pill fills an empty bra quite nicely
and gives you the freedom
 to fuck up your body.

Serious pepper is two bodies rubbing
together beneath the sheets
making more noise than love.

Serious pepper is the grinding
of black on black or black on white
or white on black.

The man, to a weighed down heart
is a way out
until the lump in the throat

means you can't talk about
what you want to. Serious
pepper. You're toothless again

learning to speak your first words.
Mummy. Daddy. Joined in bed
how could you predict the future?

III. You eat pepper soup on Monday
and baked potatoes on Tuesday.
Wednesday morning they say

'Nigerian English!
Sounds like you have an identity problem
people will think you're mixed race!'

Well that's not far from the truth, is it
but I compromise with 'Nigerian British'
'British' reminding me so much

of greed. Of Nigeria swallowed up
of Scotland   Wales   Ireland.
It will always grate, British, often

an umbrella term that means 'English'...
And it's raining now
hard like it always does

PATIENCE AGBABI

and I fry a plantain
and think of making love
for want of a better term.

Belongings are unimportant
but belonging
is . Everyone's born

no-one's found until
they find themselves hurting
in the back of the throat.

JOYOTI GRECH

Militant Roti

Haldi / Jeera / Garam Masala
Bhindi / Brinjal / Dal

- spice & sabzi keep my soul / whole
mighty magic
frying up together
for my friends & family
to eat together

reminds me of the reason
why I'm also / mad as hell
& not just
safe & strong /from smells & flavours to savour

because the day after there's
sniffing in the air & strange looks
cast toward the frying pan / the fridge / the
rubbish in the corner / & the voice of england
asks

where is that smell
coming from / is it some special kind of
spices / that you use
& is there some special kind of
way that you can / get RID of it?

Because finally that's what you want to do is
finally

get RID of it
like you want to
get RID of / us / reminding you that this is
NOT the land of hope & glory / that this is
NOT EITHER the land of the free

but it's / reminding you about your own
EMBARRASSING
history / oh how
EMBARRASSING

we ran an empire once / just like the
shop on the corner / nation of shopkeepers
we used to be / & it was my dad / in those days
who ran the shop on the corner
but look who runs it now
I ask you - it was never like that in the
Good Old Days
I've got nothing against them mind you
I just wish they'd all
GO HOME
Well look around you mr. voice of england
I am home / long time / before you
discovered my cooking
my history
my geography
my life

and I refuse to be
yr. educator

yr. mother
yr. lover or
yr. wife
I refuse to be yr.
guilt trip

but it's so embarrassing for you to
remember that / just like it's so
embarrassing to you / when I
eat with my fingers
oh how uncivilized
& suddenly
it's a gesture of / militant barbarism
& I'm only doing it / to embarrass you
not because it tastes good
but only to remind you / of your
horrible history
suddenly
eating roti with my fingers / is a
gesture of radical resistance
- not because it
tastes so good

2 fingers & a roti to yr. own
liberal paranoia
2 fingers & a roti to yr. own
xenophobia
to all yr. fancy words
2 fingers & a roti to yr. own
rotting racism.

JOYOTI GRECH

Sleeping in my Sleep
(Weavers Fields May 90)

i see you / sleeping in my sleep

in the face of hate
we have to throw back / something
stronger

in the face of hate
we react with
unity / or something
that looks like it

in the face of hate it's
anger
fuelling our fight against
the ugliness / the ignorance
the violence / that keeps us separated
by more than a police line
by more than a single / straining
Rottweiller

it's
anger
keeping us / alive and spitting
keeping us / TOGETHER

against them / whatever else
we are amongst ourselves

but after
in the quiet
& a few steps / hours away

i need to see you / sleeping in my sleep
rub away the fear & hatred
fill the gaps of hate with love
eliminate their ugliness with
our own sweet preciousness
life-affirming
hate-erasing
UNITY / with URGENCY

we need to see that we're / still breathing
skin to skin &
flesh to flesh
check each little inch
get our heart & lungs up close
loving-up with each other
getting close to each other
share some sweet and special
something / hot and sweet
deep inside
we have to get so close to
find it / loving-up

& afterwards
sleeping then / eating potato salad
wanting to cry

it's not just
the loving-up / that made us
sleep so heavy

remembering / the hours & the steps that went before
                    / the urgency & need

i'll go on remembering / the reasons why
i'll go on seeing you / sleeping in my sleep

Black Bucket

i'm Black
but that's a bucket
that only catches some of
what i am / the whole of it is
more than that
it's a cloudburst / a downpour
a rainstorm / an endless monsoon
falling all over

the first drop fell in Hamida's house
on Eskaton Road / the day she told my Ma
- it's what you wanted -

& my Ma thought Oh / unclearly
because she wouldn't have minded
a boy or a girl
but labour is a lengthy job and she
wasn't about to quibble over such
a minor detail / Doctor
hand it over anyway

so i was born / a red crab
with sex & skin & flesh & bones / my own

& that's the way it stayed
with 1 or 2 breaks along the way / other
people tried to
stake a claim / or 2 / or 4 or more but
where i come from (you understand)
there is no concept of private property / exclusive
possession so
the clutches of their belongings
soon slipped off my slick skin

& it's been changing / moving / growing
ever since / with all my
heart & soul & mind inside

& all the changing / clashing / blending
colours of the outside packaging
depending on the eyesight or the

Joyoti Grech

spectacles
of whoever's looking
- i learnt to leave that off my
own agenda
- i'm no optician
i'm no chameleon either
i'm constant / i'm constantly cooking
& my menu is good
never mind the ingredients / every
time i try to write about
the origins of me
 my pen starts wandering the
world / gets bored with tracing trees
runs away from roots / would rather
travel forwards than back
& that's true

but this time here i learnt
another truth a 2nd / everlasting time:
that forwards is not always a
predictable direction &
diversions are often not
what they seem to be
refuelling is a necessary occupation
& round routes are
mostly most fulfilling
all round / you see
what i'm saying

you can call it travel or
struggle or progressive growth
you can give it one of many names
            in almost any language
whatever it is / it's all a part of
me
& some of it is
in the bucket / brimming over
& more of it is falling all over
& even more of it is steaming
upwards
into the latest little latent
drops / getting ready to fall / all
over again

DEBJANI CHATTERJEE

The Piercing Sound

Being Black British spells ethnicity
and complicated nationality,
home-grown brown sahibs with identity
disorders like dual heredity
that diagnose a schizophrenic condition.
(The piercing sound of black incarceration.)

Of course, the empirewallahs were pucca sahibs
who drank chhota pegs on verandahs of white clubs,
Anglo-India was / colourful and contained,
like kedgeree or rich mulligatawny soup
- no problems then. It bred some eccentrics, odd bods,
mad dogs and Englishmen out in the noonday sun.
The damned climate, the tropical heat, were at odds
- it was never the men by whom the Raj was won.

Here when our Rasta brother says: "I
and I suffer in Babylon," why
then, he loads ammunition for those
who would cart him away, lock him up
for the safety of society,
and administer drugs, of the state-approved kind
- to control behaviour, not to enter his mind.
Minority protest crushed through deportation,
but some Black British are here to stay, though confined.
(The piercing sound of black incarceration.)

DEBJANI CHATTERJEE

The unmanageable black man is a mad man
is a bad man is a black man, logic rotates.
So our people are labelled mad. Indeed there is
a certain madness, not of the mind alone, but
deep nurtured in our very souls. Yes, we have roots
here and roots there, and embrace routes to everywhere
- one love for one world. Across continents is heard
the piercing sound of black incarceration.

Yes, we are mad. Mad at our children's exclusions,
deprivations, expulsions, incarcerations
in behaviour problem centres, sin bins, units
for special needs - apartheid at an early age.
Mad at the harrassment black families suffer:
single parents, joint families, we are never
the norm. Mad to see our elders cast aside when
the mother country no longer needs their presence.
Mad that our young inhabit dole queues of despair
Mad to be told to integrate, lose our cultures
and languages, throw away the chips from shoulders
splintering under the post-colonial burden.
Mad at the many injustices around us.
Mad at the inequalities we now endure.
Yes, our pride and anger stem from reality.
Our madness is a certain sign of sanity
piercing the sound of black incarceration.

Debjani Chatterjee

Primary Purpose

No matter though you're British born,
All know you are an Asian woman.
No matter what your generation,
You will always be an immigrant.
So when that day of dreams arrives,
Let me tell you how they'll solemnise -
Courtesy of the Home Office -
Holy matrimony modern style.
Always politely paternal between you,
Double checking the ink stains of marriage sheets,
"Primary purpose of marriage - immigration"
Is forever the Home Office incantation.
You must prove otherwise, being guilty without trial.
You must learn that yours is a union
Entered into lightly, only witness
All the to-ing and fro-ing of families
Negotiating flimsy alliances.
The Law's rich dowry of heartbreak
Or repatriation is freely given.
The lingering glances on either side
Of the Home Office chaperon,
Yearlong arrangements, in the twinkling of an eye,
At the stroke of a Home Office Pen,
Add up to a marriage of convenience -
Of course an immigrant's, casually fixed.
Your marriage is a life long separation

Of two statistics, one male, one female,
Stretching letters across continents
Till they become habitual silence
That speaks of aloneness of body, mind and spirit,
Mingling with the sorrow of Asian thousands.
God's primitive will has no place
In a civil and civilised ceremony.
 Here the Home Office presides at Asian nuptials,
The unknown guest, invisible, almighty,
Tut, tears are so emotional,
So typically Asian, feminine, futile.
Sister, may your understanding grow
Of your alien status
And deepen with the years.
You are married and yet single - naturally!
Are you not British and yet black?
Learn to sing of thwarted love and broken home,
Old slave songs of civil liberty denied.
All know there is no love in Asian marriages.
The Law knows you for your family's chattel,
So companionship and children do not fit the picture.
At least you will not reproduce
More Asian females to breathe this air of freedom, and fair play.
It will be easy to love, honour and be faithful
Until the Law does you part.
Exercise your fond imagination
To love some fading memory,
To hold some fleeting vision,

DEBJANI CHATTERJEE

Not knowing if he's better or worse,
Richer or poorer, in sickness or in health.
To this you pledge yourself before the Home Office.
The rubber stamps you rubber man and wife.
Those whom the immigration law has kept apart
Let no one join together.
"Primary purpose of marriage - immigration"
Is forever the Home Office incantation.
The Law is your protection, your guidance and blessing,
The Law is your jailer, its rod and staff injure you.
Peers of the realm, is this justice?
Big brother, when will this nightmare end?

Southall

Oh dear Southall
didn't we struggle to call you home
But you, alone gave birth to us
and weren't we strong in you once

In your arms we ran and played,
and then,
God, how your streets aroused us
But we came away
We couldn't control you
We couldn't let you control us

And so we struggled, we discovered
We came to find 'our place'
and you are now so culturally accessible
and we are of course, so safe

Oh dear Southall
Coming to you now still bolts the system
and why not? Maybe it should
We have no right to call you ours:-
Maybe we should have stayed

Oh, and as the Braodway looms, and
the traffic jams start,
Some part of our naive hearts

still calls out to seek refuge
but too much has passed between us

How is it that you rule us?
We fought to leave
We struggle to return
How indeed you fool us

STORME WEBBER

to be a woman in new york city

to be a woman in new york city
is to be a warrior
these days
i'm so sick of violence
i'm ready to kill somebody
like every two-footed dog
i heard say bitch this year
& laugh/yes every mother's son
why waste the oxygen?
consider the greenhouse effect
& all this so called expression
of popular culture
that uses me for an asswipe
or a jack off rag
may the poison you disperse
so freely/choke you slowly
while mr. t fucks you up every orifice
(wit no grease)
& i'll play those records LOUD in yr ear
yeah motherfucker i house *you*
you in MY HUT NOW
little mister man
you who are not my daddy
my brother my son or lover
MIND YR BIZNESS
my hair my ass my tiddies

my girlfriend are MINE
you know you cd be LIVING
instead of barking & scratching
on street corners
whyn't you STAND UP
let go of yr dick
& be a human being.

"blues for star eyes"

love sugar is the dance we left
in the middle of
we forgot (or we thought) we forgot
the steps/so we stepped off
the scene leaving anything but a clean
break not even a heart or two
mine waz ripped raw to ragged seams
unspent full grown love running out
in every all kind of direction/chaos
of emotion we thought it better to close
the door tried to push all untidiness
inna closet/& move on
& on we & time went/i have rambled
you stayed put/found stability not without struggle
our feelings/still alive sometimes ached like a missing
limb/as though we cd still feel with them even tho
amputation waz complete hearts have memories like elephants
specially for soulmates/even when they mug yr vulnerabilities

leave you oozing & raging in some dank street
i can't help it/yr image tattooed inside my eyelids
fingertips/mouth/i can't though sure if i cd
i wd even wrap you carefully/peacefully/in a blk silk
cloth/& leave you somewhere/vibeless vague as detail becomes
but too much remains & i don't have any storage space
you see i really move around too much to carry this much on with
i carry my home/of memory & dream on my back & there's not
so much room inside this shell/i need more space for the new
& i'm not so sure of these other steps we trying to make up here
soon as i figure out how/i'm a haveta evict you
i'm a haveta peel back my eyelids/trade fingertips wit
somebody that never touched you
surely somewhere/another mouth/new eyes
surely somewhere/a cosmos where we never met.

Faith

Faith is the springboard to eternity. "The substance of things hoped for; the evidence of things not seen." If we stand tall it is because we stand upon the heads of our ancestors (as they stood upon theirs). What has linked these souls, this continuum of survival but *faith*?

We struggle we stand up & fight for our rights not just because we are angry and contentious.
We fight for what we believe in: the future in all its glorious possibility & the sweet fresh air of freedom.
We know by our faith and by our actions we move forward.

L<small>INDA</small> K<small>ING</small>

Blues Song For Rodney King

Rewind Rodney King
Rewind Rodney King
Rewind Rodney King
each time the button pressed cable
cabling sound intermezzo
I heard your Stradivarius cry!
White lighting/contrabasso
bowed waves bridging the ivory night.

Boy! brother man bust/blood/Louis Armstrong/bomb
beads poured down in our living room.
Love and laughter froze up
on a lacquered lake
leaking down our faces
unrehearsed/saxophone/scalding/savage/scar
Blue song/we sang for our Native son

sent my tuning fork tintinnabulum
tom tommed my bongo/tamborined
my tabla/released my Centaurian Rhapsody.
They beat up a Shepherd that day
Scherzo/Salmagundi/Obligatto
Through the eye of Cleopatra's needle
I caress the Cobra.
Kiss the Coca Cola commercial goodbye!

The police shot a line/the courtroom slime
a verdict signal/for a showdown.
Summer Symbols/Missiles/No Sermons
Yo shouting Yo/Yo showdown Yo/Showdown
on the slime.

A Chrysalis moon droned on the hive of a Hornets' nest.
Bluenote Canon/televised
the Choral rhythm of a nation.
Nation touching Nation/Antiphony/Dithyramb.
This attack on Caliph released the Assegai spear
to cauterize the burning tirade.

Prevail Rajah! Reload the rhythm relentlessly/Radical radiance.
Coconuts fall in rapid succession/echoing/concentric heartbeats.
Salmagundi/Obligatto/tintinnabulum
Bongos tamborined my Tabla
Cicada drones my backbone.

"We hold these truths to be self evident.
All men are created equal."
Rephrase power to the people!
Return/reverberate/ride the stormridge
Robin/Hood/Roe.

Delilah Demerara decipher the double talk
Double up/disconnect/do up the drum beat/dusk dawn.
New Wave son/Nicotine Nightowls/New Wave Nirvana Freaks

blend a Lullaby exposition/recapitulating/Yakety Yak
Yakety Yak/Don't talk back.
Our Yeti Bessie Smith's Angels
know the true story of King Kong.

Shift the turmoil/The people have been fermenting on figs.
Fist not the raised fist of the sixties/Flood Omega!
Where the rainbow ends/Ochre my love/a new frontier.
On the edge/on the house/on the move/Ormolu
Good sharp reception/ounce for ounce syncopation.
Purify the oxygen!

Kiss the Coca Cola commercial goodbye!
Kiss the Coca Cola commercial goodbye!
Kiss the Coca Cola commercial goodbye!

I Am A Poem

I am a poem
written in anger
I can comfort
or cause u pain
you've nought to lose
all to gain
so read me
fill your soul
I'm a poem
silent like a stream
running to the open
sea to be free
touching coast to coast
in any tongue
sometimes written. sometimes
a song of liberation
or frustration at
a corrupt system
I'm a poem
take me. read me
fill your soul
I'm a poem
in my words
I can hush a baby
or start a war
I'm a poem telling

the world of the truth
which nothing
is new
I'm a poem
sometimes happy
sometimes blue
I'm a poem
I was written for
you. take me
read me!
fill your soul
I'm a poem
written in anger
silent with scorn
I am the writing
on the wall
what is covered
will be exposed
for the eye to see
take me! read me
fill your soul
I am the word on the wind
blowing along
I am a poem
sometimes sullen
sometimes bold
I can be smutty
erotic

stinging hard
like the fruit of the earth
I am the poem of nature
I am the poem for all
nations
who want to be free
take these words to you
from me
take me! read me!
fill your soul
take me read me
fill your soul

BROTHER RESISTANCE

Is It Safe

Is it safe
to be yourself in ah society
where priority is on pose an posture
where tryin to be like somebody else
is all dat matter
is it safe
to be strong in a society
where preference is offered to weakness
an courage is referred by many
as nothing but madness
is it safe
is it safe
to say No
in ah 'yes man' society
to seek truth
in ah land of lies and deception
is it safe
is it safe
to seek justice
where iniquity reign
is it safe
to live wid ah love for freedom
in de midst of all oppression
and do nothing about dat feeling
is it safe
is it safe
is it safe...eh?

BROTHER RESISTANCE

Can I Get Ah Witness

now dis here lyric comin from de heart an soul
an is ah special request to all de oppress an dispossess
thruout de world

But look at my crosses
is you wey drain meh resources
an now yuh makin policy
to enforce my poverty
an like beggar look we knockin on yuh door
we pot a fire but it empty for sure
we hear de strain but we cyar take no more
now we life ha no meanin
we only wukin an scruntin

Yuh send slave drivers
economic advisors
monetary prescription
to promote starvation
so independence doh mean ah ting
when yuh country like ah puppet on ah string
yuh call de tune to make we dance an swing
now we life ha no meanin
we unemployed an scruntin

dis colonial legacy
is ah persistent poverty

BROTHER RESISTANCE

like when ah bread ha no butter
like when ah sheep ha no pasture
yuh pauperize an demoralize
devastate an dehumanize
ah tell yuh people open yuh eyes
'cause yuh life ha no meanin
we only wukin an scruntin
       wukin an scruntin

is ah grand conspiracy
perpetuatin slavery
control we economee
an frustrate we destiny
wid self reliance an togedderness
we as ah people could find happiness
we want to live an not merely exist
gi we life ah new meanin
no more wukin an scruntin
no more wukin an scruntin

Yuh see de IMF takin advantage
ah want ah witness
yuh see de IMF dig out we eye
ah want ah witness
yuh see de IMF leave we in bondage
ah want ah witness
yuh see de IMF force we to cry
ah want ah witness...

ah want ah witness oh
ah want ah witness

Yuh see de IMF bleedin we country
ah want ah witness
but look de IMF jook out we eye
ah want a witness
testify fo me
testify fo me
de IMF...international mafia

Attila The Stockbroker

Market Sektor One
(Summer 1990)

Another new year and too much beer and goodbye to the wall
But now there's only disappointment, nothing left at all
The dreams we marched and fought for have faded and turned sour
The cabbage is a king now, it's Helmut's finest hour
And on the streets the people want it 'as seen on TV'
And a big bunch of bananas is a sign that you are free
It's just begun - Market Sektor One

As in the East they talk about a future bold and new
a thousand Western businessmen are celebrating too
the vultures are all circling 'cos there's money to be made
a multinational carve-up, a bank to be obeyed
and now the old, rich foreigners make claims on every hand
'you're living in my house, mein Herr, you're farming on my land'
It's time to run - Market Sektor One

Is that all we were fighting for?
Bananas and sex-shops, nothing more?
Welcome to the Western dream
Welcome to the cheap labour scheme

The whole of Europe's changing - Big Brother's on the run
It could just be a brand new age of freedom has begun
But freedom doesn't bow it's head to some financier's will
And Europe is our common home - not some gigantic till

So send the money grabbers riding off into the sun
And take your assets in your own hands, answerable to none
Then we'll have fun and justice will be done....

This Is Free Europe

Dead of night in Carpentras
Brings the ghosts from the days of Vichy
Broken windows in the high street
Swastikas in the cemetery
Blond young men on a Dresden evening
Beer and loathing on their breath
Ten to one like their cowardly fathers
Arms outstretched in the sign of death

Chorus:
If it takes a voice then shout the truth
If it takes a hand then hold them back
If it takes a fist then strike them down
From Cable Street to Hoyerswerda
Pamyat, Schönhuber and Le Pen -
This is Free Europe...never again!

Afternoon in a Soviet city
Now they don't even need to hide
Blue shirt thugs advertise their pogroms
None are arrested, none are tried
'Pamyat' means 'a memory' -

ATTILA THE STOCKBROKER

What memories for these Russian nazis?
Children killed in front of their mothers
Human skin turned into lampshades

CHORUS

Once more we see the darkness in the European soul
As the chains fall there comes an awful beast
His eyes are staring, and there is hell upon his brow -
Oscar, Francois, Gregor, Tanya listen to me now...

CHORUS

I'm a Jew in Carpentras
I'm a Jew in that Soviet city
I'm an Asian in the East End
I'm a Cuban in East Germany
Don't tell me it doesn't concern us
It's not something to ignore
They are feeding on our apathy -
That's how it began before...

Chorus:
If it takes a voice then shout the truth
If it takes a hand then hold them back
If it takes a fist then strike them down
From Cable Street to Hoyerswerda
Pamyat, Schönhuber and Le Pen -
This is Free Europe ...never again!

Mihalakis

At school,
They gave us all kinds a names,
Dished out every lesson,
On playing pitches
And over stormy dining tables.
They called me many names,
I had more nicknames than the year has days,
More nicknames than the sun has rays.
Them call me...
"Colour !"
Call me Paki, Diego, Whop, Spik and Darkie.
Them call me...
"Class !"
Said I should work like my parents,
Long hard hours - sweating buckets, present - past.
Them call me...
"Intelligence !"
Said I was linguistically backward,
Taught me rugby and football
And maintained that my maths and history were
"Dodgy and awkward".
Them also call me...
"Culture !"
Said I was skitzofrenik,
Trapped in some kind of bi-cultural panic,
Lost in Britain and not proud of it.

HAJI-MIKE

Call me colour,
Call me class,
Call me all kinds of
Fucking Raasss!!!

But them never called me,
Mihalakis,
By my name,
For that
Was all
I ever
Asked.

Intifadah

I tell you not a tale
Daughters of Palestine
Sons of Palestine
I too know the taste of
pain unleashed
Like vinegar darting across
a gaping wound
Like the sting of
a slave driver's whip
Stalking my sisters' barren back
   way
     down
        there in Mississippi
Like the silent wail of
a Guatemalan orchid
as the US adviser
jerkily plucks its petals
on the lawns of
the Presidential Palace

      I too know
   the tangy taste of pain
Yet, by the sturdy olive tree
  I stand, stubborn
When the whirlwind unfurls
menacing,

threatening to uproot Palestine

I too know
   the taste of pain
I was there in
   KAFR Kassem
       Deir Yassin
       Sabra Shatila
Perhaps you saw me there
     Perhaps too in the smile of
     an eight year old Arab child
     as she hurled her first stone
on the face of an Israeli soldier

I too was there
   in Lebanon
choking in the fumes
by a pile of empty
   South African shells.

Did you hear my throttled sobs
    at the siege of Beirut ?
Did you hear me curse
    as my watery eyes,
      bulbs of my being,
        time bound
    raced back to Dachau
        Belsen
        Auschwitz

AHMED SHEIKH

Can this be
        I asked
the deed of the orphaned
    sons and daughters of
        the holocaust?

Can this be
        the deed of the orphaned Jew
        to whom Lord Balfour
            and the United Nations
            bartered my birthright?

I tell you not a tale
        Daughters of Palestine
        Sons of Palestine
I too know
the taste of pain unleashed
Like the shame of
an Arab child
having to write
the word Israel
on the map of
her native land

Like the sorrow of
        Samih al Qasim
burning to bake a poem
    in his homeland

AHMED SHEIKH

Like our names,
stolen
Glorious names
Names whose ring
speak the language of
    the Gods and the Goddesses
Galilee, Nazareth,
Shafr'Amr, Umm el Fahm
Golan Heights, Gaza
Jerusalem, Bethlehem

I too am Palestine
    the ascending lisp of
        a distended catapult
           in Soweto
I am the voice of Haiti
    Mighty Haiti
    Black Haiti
I routed Europe's armies
My palms reach out to
    the Native American
    the Arawak
    the Eritrean
    the Armenian
    the Saharoui
    the Aborigine
    the Irish
    and the Azanian

and the Untouchable
     and the Wretched of
       the Earth.

I too am Palestine
   the morning dew
    drops drip.   Dripping
    Liquid seed
The rainbow
  clinging at
  the mouth of the cataract
The blade of exile
    mangles my insides
    but I have buried my heart
      And my umbilical chord
    deep at the foot of
   a young olive tree
And I have lent my songs
spun in the homeland
    like the finest bridal cloth,
   to migratory birds
   to drop over the barbed wires
   and the rooftops of Palestine
I too know
   the joy of living
The aroma of the homeland
   I too like
to visit old friends

pick an orange
    a date or two
in Grandfather's field
sit at the feet of
    old Aunt Fatima
delightfully
    sucking her wrinkled cheeks
whilst narrating
her favourite story
    how she once
    with her bare hands
    strangled an Israeli soldier
who raped and killed
    her seven year old
      Cousin Fadwa

Let the PLO flag
    fly high in Palestine
    as it does in my heart
      she said
Let Kalashnikovs
    sing in unison
and the chorus of cannons
merge with the symphony of
            bullets.

The homeland
    shall grieve no more

Daughters of Palestine
    Sons of Palestine
We shall ululate pearls of sound
    as only the homeland folks
        know how
We shall knead bread
    for those to come
and then we shall dance
    the rain dance

Intifadah
    I too am Palestine
Intifadah
    No hint of fading!
Intifadah
    Particle of sand
Intifadah
    Atom of hope
    Split to infinity
Intifadah
Tremor of the earth
    Tremor of the earth
Intifadah
    Red ink
    on Lord Balfour's sleeve
Intifadah
    Ray of light
    in the fertile heart of

Palestine.
I swear, I tell you not a tale
Daughters of Palestine
Sons of Palestine
I too am Palestine
I swear
on the greying beard of
Yasser Arafat
I too am Palestine
on the shoulders of
the United Leadership of
Intifadah
I too am Palestine
on the potent pen of
Fadwa Touqan
Mahmud Darwish
Samih al Qasim
I too am Palestine
On the defiant gaze of
a Gaza child
I swear
I too am Palestine
INTIFADAH
Weave us a garland of
bullets.

Now Is The Time

Time to be practical,
An analysis of the spiritual.
Overstand the political,
And defeat the hypocritical.

Conciousise the ill.
Grab a little skill.
Learn to sweeten 'the pick me up pill.'

Hail Africa's contribution.
But not Europe's prostitution.
Nor Amerikkka's moralistic destitution.

De-ignorise the ignorant.
Wake up the dormant.
Tear down the horrendous Houses of Parliament.

Time to be positive.
No, don't get negative.
Even though our leaders are in need of a laxative.
De-pessimise the mind.
Optimise the will.
And remind the people that in life
Nothing stands still.

NOW IS THE TIME.

Nick Toczek

FINANCIAL AFFAIRS

We were merely exchanging stock.
Love really clearly came as a shock.
I said: "If you feel like I feel
I think we should go for a business deal."
She said I should urge her.
I tried the take-over bit.
She said: "You sexist shit!
I meant a merger."
I said: "Not me, our kid,
when I'm right on the verge of
a major bid for you."

All I wanted was the company.
But whooo! True passion'll
take you over like a multinational.

She said: "You're too late, mate,
if you're mid-way through
cos I already did what you plan to do
meaning I put in my bid for you
and I just spoke to my broker...
I got controlling shares
in you and your heirs
in perpetuity —
so it's you that belongs to me."

All I wanted was the company.
But whooo! True passion'll
take you over like a multinational,
strip your assets and strip your cash'n'all.

She said: "Down on one knee...!
Say those three little words to me."
I said: "Which three?" She said: "Think!"
I said: "Well now, let me see...
hmmm... I know! Rio Tinto Zinc."
Well, she went frantic.
She'd never heard anything so romantic —

Woah! True passion'll
take you over like a multinational.
All I wanted was the company, y'see.
But whooo! True passion'll
turn you irrational,
make you brash'n'all...
take you over
take you over
take you over like a multinational.

NICK TOCZEK
11-19/6/'88

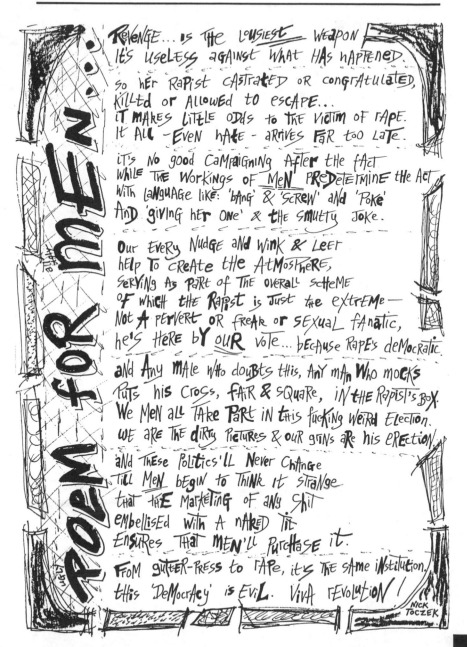

Revenge... is the lousiest weapon.
It's useless against what has happened.
So her rapist castrated or congratulated,
killed or allowed to escape...
it makes little odds to the victim of rape.
It all - even hate - arrives far too late.

It's no good campaigning after the fact
while the workings of MEN predetermine the act
with language like: 'bang' & 'screw' and 'poke'
and 'giving her one' & the smutty joke.

Our every nudge and wink & leer
help to create the atmosphere,
serving as part of the overall scheme
of which the rapist is just the extreme—
not a pervert or freak or sexual fanatic,
he's here by OUR vote... because rape's democratic.

And any male who doubts this, any man who mocks
puts his cross, fair & square, in the rapist's box.
We men all take part in this fucking weird election.
We are the dirty pictures & our guns are his erection.

And these politics'll never change
till men begin to think it strange
that the marketing of any shit
embellished with a naked tit
ensures that MEN'll purchase it.

From gutter-press to rape, it's the same institution.
This 'democracy' is evil. Viva revolution!

NICK
TOCZEK

191

B<small>RIDGIT</small> B<small>ARD</small>

La Isla Concreta

Yo soy en Espania in search of el Sol
Yo voy out of season to get away from
it, all
So in the daytime I try a
sun bed on la playa
in the hope that my body
will turn mucho brown

pero I did not remember
that in April and September
hay muchas touristas
que fly into town
quando los caballeros
y los ambre soleros
come out like iguanas
to worship the sun

they drive you bananas
they bite like pirhanas
they promise manyanas
and tomorrow they're gone

Out on the street it's
Hola Senorita
your eyes are so sweet
I'd like to give you what for

but I'm sick to the teeth
of being eyed up like meat
so I vote with my feet
and I say Beat It Senor

The signs say
Hola y Buen as Vistas
Bienvenida las Touristas
Mira la Isla
y las vistas del Mar
pero no es possible
ver la rock formation
for la Urbanisation
has gone mucho too far
the place is full of touristas
it's a government feat
but all los alredadores
are made of concrete
It's true that
Mi historia de Mallorca
is not exactly Lorca
pero es la verdad

ELEAN THOMAS

The Tourist

A side-walk cafe bordering
the square of the Metropolis
        Athens Greece

Elite designer-clothes shop
crunch shoulders with
American-international banks
fine-gold jewellery
beaten silver
authentic-Greek history porcelain
bazaars
cathedral grand with
piped-organ music
looks down flea-market
Greek-tourist souvenir
street

Any currency will do
in the Metropolis
        Athens Greece

    Two sisters
equally peasant-fat
from constant wheat
and too-little meat
waddle into the square

of the Metropolis
    Athens Greece

Both laden down
with stuffed shoulder-bags
exquisitely hand-embroidered
    table-cloths
in white and beige
Start from the top of flea-market street
in the Metropolis
    Athens Greece

Stand uncertainly
try to catch even one eye
of strolling tourists
from America and the EEC
in the Metropolis
    Athens Greece

Perhap think this tourist
looks like us
or perhaps because this tourist
is seated at the side-walk cafe
and is already looking at them
so their eyes do not need
to catch those eyes
of this tourist
in the Metropolis
    Athens Greece

ELEAN THOMAS

One Grecian sister approaches
    the tourist
whispers low
so the big-shop owners cannot hear
    Good Pretty For Table
    Me Mama Make
    Give You Good Price
    In Drachmas

The tourist pulls the table-cloth
much closer to her eyes and hands
the tourist feels and sees
through the ten-thousand intricate
    stitches
the Grecian sisters' Mama
in the cramped peasant hut

Needle into cloth
needle out of cloth
in a round of nights and days
thumb and forefinger
swollen and raw
with a billion needle pricks
aching head and darked eyes
tears a-clogging the nose
from hours and hours
of fixed stare
on white and beiged thread

aluminium-iron needle
lips moving
forever stuck
in a rhythm of eternal prayers
to count and count each stitch
that must of necessity form
    the pattern
of each exquisite table-cloth

One stich too much!
must start all over again

This table-cloth must be perfectly-made
for the tourists
in the Metropolis
    Athens Greece

> *Give you good price in drachmas*
> *You have dollars?*
> *Fifty dollars*
> *No? How much you have?*
> *Tell me*
> *I make good price*
> *Thirty dollars?*
> *How much drachmas you have?*
> *I make good price*
> *No drachmas ?*

Then twenty-five dollars
Me Mama need
She got no food
I give you
for even
Twenty dollars
or whatever drachmas
you have

The tourist knows
the thread alone
to make this exquisite table-cloth
comes first of all from India
to cotton mills of Liverpool
then to multinational companies
of United States of America
to junior partners in the EEC
arriving at last
at Athens Greece
for more than twenty dollars

So the Mama's labour is as
        for nothing
when the table-cloth reaches
the Metropolis
of the square
in historical
        Athens Greece

The tourist does not speak
in the language
of the Grecian peasant sister
but the tourist hopes
her eyes alone
can talk to this sister
standing at the side-walk cafe
in the Metropolis
      Athens Greece

The tourist sends a message
through the pupils of her eyes

On the other side of the world
      the message read
her Mama too
embroiders table-cloths
in cramped two-room shack
at the foot of Wareika Hills
Caribbean island
of Jamaica

Needle into calico cloth
needle out of calico cloth
in a round of nights and days
thumb and forefinger
swollen and raw
with a billion needle pricks

aching head and darked eyes
tears a-clogging the nose
from kerosene lamp-dark
and hours upon hours
of fixed stare
on calico table-cloths
multi-coloured threads
aluminium-iron needle
lips moving
forever stuck
in a rhythm of eternal prayers
to count and count each stitch
that must of necessity form
     the pattern
of each exquisite table-cloth

One stitch too much!
must start all over again

This table-cloth must be perfectly-made
for the tourists
in the Metropolis
     Montego Bay Jamaica
where her Mama's labour is as
     for nothing
just like the labour
of the Grecian sisters' Mama

The tourist said
through the movement of her eyes
        and hands
Please do understand
Had I one million dollars
or 100 million drachmas
I would give it without hesitation
for your Mama's table-cloth
in the Metropolis
of Athens ancient Greece

The eyes communicate
across language history
geography
between far-sited metropolises
of Montego Bay Jamaica
and the square of Athens Greece

For the Grecian sister smiled
saw and understood
that within the depths
of the tourist's closed purse
was only fifty drachmas
and two American dollars
just enough for a cup of coffee
and a single open-faced sandwich
in the Metropolis
        Athens Greece

ELEAN THOMAS

The Grecian sister's eyes
    replied
to the tourist sitting at the side-walk cafe
in the Metropolis
    Athens Greece

    Take heart my love
    for when we succeed to get
    all the daughters and sons
    of Our Mamas
    in full control
    of all the world
    Our Mamas' labour
    will be as dear
    as life itself
    in ALL Metropolises.

What's Happening

What's happening
You'll know what's happening
when you see Pedro the poet
selling condoms and poetry books
and hear the man of god
choking on his sexual contradictions
you'll know what's happening
when you see computers going to sleep on
shoulders of their secretaries and
hear workers dismantling governments
in Europe
in South Africa
you'll know what's happening

What's happening
An intellectual is marching around like
a great humanitarian but won't pay his
child support that's what's happening
And on the lower east side of New York City
a Doris Day look alike is imitating the voice of
Louis Satchmo Armstrong while
the minister of unneccessary information
gets his hair curled
That's what happening
The musicians are making facial expressions acting
like they're really playing something complex
                              and are not

That's what's happening
& me? Me?
I have already dropped a half inch of
slobber on a certain line
I have already placed parachutes on
two mountains of paper
OK   It's only one word in three hours
but look at you
look at you
Your job is to be a singing raisin
He's a dancing cornflake
You're a smiling commode
She's a walking roll of toilet tissue
He falls on the beach like
a sack of empty bullet shells
She's forced to sit like a ground based
missile interceptor in the tourist area while
commander in chief invades Panama and
shoots Panamanians democratically to
enforce human rights and burn up another flag
That's what's happening
And there are other drug dealers butting
                              heads in the dark
other equal opportunity killers on
                              the horizon
other fraudulent financiers manipulating money
                              and doing the hand jive
other corrupt hotel chain owners with

nice clothes and dirty drawers
That's what's happening
Meanwhile
the meter "maids" are still giving parking tickets
and the gospel singers are still taking cliches
                              and beating them to death
and the xmas tree crews are out discovering the
deepest hole of their consciousness in the donut shop
and little ladies in long coats are walking in
competition with big ladies in tight pants
and here we are between the emergency exit of
                              a closing bank
and the ambulance entrance of an ageing nuclear reactor
waiting for the economic recovery of our dreams
and that's what's happening
that's what happening

Push Back The Catastrophes

I don't want a drought to feed on itself
through the tattooed holes in my belly
I don't want a spectacular desert of
charred stems & rabbit hairs
in my throat of accumulated matter
I don't want to burn and cut through the forest
like a greedy mercenary drilling into
sugar cane of the bones

Push back the advancing sands
the polluted sewage
the dust demons   the dying timber
the upper atmosphere of nitrogen
push back the catastrophes

Enough of the missiles
the submarines
the aircraft carriers
the biological weapons
No more sickness   sadness   poverty
exploitation   destabilization
illiteracy and bombing
Let's move toward peace
toward equality and justice
that's what I want

To breathe clean air
to drink pure water to plant new crops
to soak up the rain to wash off the stink
to hold this body and soul together in peace
that's it
Push back the catastrophers

These days...

These days I converse with death
behind a funeral procession of ideas
a horse drawn cart gallops away with
coffins draped in bleeding shrouds

The funeral is postponed
I tease death
for keeping his landlord waiting

The earth yawns
its apertures stretch their rectangular
shapes in symmetrical lines
an epidemic of rash
moves to level the earth

I converse with death these days
about a war of position
The state of affairs lies
within systems of fortresses
of earthworks

I question death's hegemony
I puzzle the dialectic of coercion and consent
death only smiles
I assess and re-assess the current situation
the balance of forces
of my organic crisis
unbalanced I threaten death with my death
He only smiles

PITIKA NTULI

For Sam Ntuli & All Those Who.....

1   I do not want to write this poem
It makes me so sad, sad
This side of despair/just
I would not mind if in its sadness
There would be a glimmer of hope
however slight
The dialectic that trudges/despite

In our teens
    loins teeming, pulsating with life
seeking little wars of pleasure
dreaming under the single eye of sunflowers
bees buzzing
little hairy silhouettes
ecstasies of honey
potentials
how would we ever guess
our country would become a giant grave?

Once more we dig
    measure soil along mounds of grief
exposed to a new wail of torrential rains
tears invisible as molten lava
my mouth is a volcanic crater silent
with word-bombs
    in the beginning was the Word

I do not want to write this poem
6000 miles away my people gather
their strength and vulnerability together
to bury that capsule of dreams

2   Other capsules wasted
               in the name of love
               of country
               of peace

I bridle the nightmare horse of anger
with a lacklustre love
               of country
               of peace

Voices of ideals whisper to me messages
of wisdom
               "do not despair
               this too will pass
               I am a footsoldier with no opinions
               only to do or die
               Voices of ideals
               have mugged me of my smiles
               The expression of my doubts"

Heaven introduces a new narrative
"Once upon a time there were revolutionaries
who never knew despair -
In the end they all died happily ever after..."

I do not want to write this poem
This scalpel that dissects my joy
my grief
in the theatre of laughter/grief

Tomorrow I will write my poem
It will begin

3   When I was sad
I danced between the rays of the sun
tip-toed on gladioli
sprang gently on to the metres of wisteria
played hide and seek
with smells of honeysuckles
to hide from pain

I opened myself up to storms of grief
dared them to wipe the dust of my hopes
from my lips
instead particles of my land
rose to kiss my lips with vibrant
promises of a new day

Diagonality

I exist in diagonality
it's a sharp uphill climb
I never reach the top
I walk around a triangle
equilateral points become the horizon.

I exist in diagonality
it's a room with two sides
the walls are tall and narrow
they fold me to confinment.

I exist in diagonality
I lie across the bed
corner to corner
filling space more readily than verticalness.

I exist in diagonality
it's the border between black and white
and it isn't grey.

I exist in diagonality
my mind tips and pours
gathering speed
momentum
inertia
my mind cascades to thought.

Maya Chowdhry

I have an idea about diagonality
and it's not straight.

I live in diagonality
and it's hard to walk
I live on the outside
beyond diagonality
I'm outside diagonality
looking in

Blood

She is a glass woman,
I see through to
the other side.   It is warm yellow,
not like her cold blue. It
stings sharp,
bites me, I
bleed. I bleed
when the moon is whole,
it wanes, I dry up
and my blood freezes. It is
icy and my blood
won't flow, I've
forgotten where it came from,
I think it's ruby
red and belongs in Scotland,
I think it's mendhi

red and belongs in India,
I think about writing
the word, I
think about writing until
I find out what colour my blood is
I think about
writing but
my blood gets in the way,
it pours heavier than
the ink on my page,
it pours and fills
the whole page,
my ink is dry and
cannot get past
two lines. Two lines more
and I'll find out,
the blue of the glass cracks.

The Sea

travels from Mandvi
to Ganga Sagar
knows no cease-fire line
or the difference between
a European and an Indian body
except the sea knows me
my brown skin
travels from Mandvi

to Ganga Sagar
unravelling around the
coasts of India
travelling from the Arabian Sea
to the Bay of Bengal
the sea travels
across oceans and does not know
that one country has ended
and another began
that the spices in supermarkets in Britain
travel
that the silk in Libertys
travels
that people
travel
except the sea finds their bodies
on her ocean bed
and unpicks their flesh
until they are bones
and only the sea knows where
she has hidden them.

ANN ZIETY

Brief Encounter

a man waits alone in a subway
with the world in his pocket

he puts his hand in his pocket
the world feels good
firm and round like a breast
he takes it out, kisses it
puts it back again

the world feels good

he keeps his hand on the world
the whole time
stroking it, patting it, keeping it in place

his hands are happy
but his eyes look for enemies

he waits for a woman to pass him in the darkness
"I'll show you the world," he says
"if you'll come home with me."

the woman looks at him and smiles
she opens her breast and takes out a heart
perfectly round
the heart turns slowly in the night

Ann Ziety

a globe

"There is more than one world," she says
and walks away

Mirror

there is this mirror
tall as a man

the man looks into it
and sees himself

the woman on the other side
looks through it
and sees man

she asks the man:
"What do I look like?"

the man, depending on his mood
tells her she looks like a monstrous whore
tells her she looks like a sweet madonna
tells her she looks like nothing at all
tells her she should alter something
and he prefers her sister anyway

after this goes on
and on
for centuries and centuries
the woman
in her rage
pushes the mirror
which smashes, jagged edged
and dangerous
on the hard ground

the shards form a lake
still and clear
and peering over the edge
hesitant, afraid
for the first time
drawing breath
she sees her self

and is staggered
by infinity

On the Darker Side of the Flyover

On the darker side of the flyover
On the crappiest part of the pavement
In a zone that was neither smokeless nor nuclear-free
Behind a dangerous chemical works
Where the coldest isobars collided

Where the distant drumming of boiler houses mingled with the icy
                                        clattering of railway carriages
Where the blue smoke borrowed the sky and never gave it back
Where pearly droplets of petrol seeped into earth and grass
Where Summer existed only in the minds of travel agents
Where the nearest bus stop was half a mile's walk
And the nearest tube was half a mile's bus ride
Where the acid rain gave the nightingales glaucoma
And the acid snow froze the hub caps of continental cars
In a land of wheel clamps and scaffolding, bulldozers and briefcases,
                                        breathalysers and chicken fried rice
Tucked away in the spaghetti squiggles of the A-Z of London
In the backside of a cul-de-sac where the bin men never came
In a street without signposts
In a suburb full of puddles
In a world turned sour
In a universe gone green
Was the space where Suzi Dishcloth found a place to live -
A flamingo-pink apartment in the half-lit Club Tropicana shish kebab
  poodle parlour fish and chip elektrofunk forests of Lego Land.

The Outrage

In the outrage of the afternoon
The velvet couch smothered the waste paper basket until it was dead
the lamp flex strangled the diningroom chairs till they croaked into splinters
The carpet arched its back and tipped over the coffee table, breaking all its legs
The electric fire scorched the potted plants until they withered neatly to nothing

The cushions chomped on smaller cushions and flubbered over the strewn

foam plastic

The vacuum cleaner chundled the ironing board
The hairdryer blew all the books out of the window
The vegetable slicer shredded the curtains to a crimplene coleslaw
The cheese grater rubbed the wallpaper to confetti
The electric toothbrush burrowed into the heart of a shrieking armchair
The eiderdown suffocated the poodle pyjama-case
The mattress hurled the blankets onto the floor as the bed booted their

soft defencelessness

The stereo unit mouthed abuse at the television screen
The drinks cabinet threw sharp-edged wine glasses at the silent ornaments
The coffee percolator spat black spit at the unarmed skirting boards
The ashtray toppled over, murking the gut of a crystal goldfish bowl

And in the midst of it all
In the midst of it all
Was Suzi Dishcloth's sadness
Beyond words
As deep as midnight
Her one unquestionable power.
With sadness she could mash a city to nothing.

Ostrich Man

I can see no evil in the world
There's nothing can make me sad
I can't see anything because
My head's inside this bag

I'm not an animal, I'm a man
I was given this by my dad
He said one day everything you will see will be yours
Then he gave me this bloody bag

The teachers gave me another
I got a further one from my mother
They gave me one at every job I had
They said 'we can see a great future for you son
Here wear this very nice bag'

But now I'm dead they say I can take it off
But though they think I'm mad
I'll show them they can't discipline me
See, I'm still wearing my bag

I showed them didn't I? I showed them.

This Land of Equal Opportunities

A patch of dirt on his mother's skirt he clings on to save his life
A passenger in her frustration dragged past the age of five
Not for him the fairy land
He's taught right and wrong by the back of the hand
His life is planned inbred at birth
The urban waste of a council estate his first taste of Mother Earth
Told to sit as soon as he could crawl
The fiction in the picture books don't fit his life at all
And his mind begins to wonder what lies behind the high school wall
His mother can't wait to placate him
She lays more sugar on his dummy
"Work harder" says his father, "you too could soon earn money."
If it wasn't so sad it might just be funny
He sees his parents lie and cheat
Then discovers the other face they displace on the street
He's being taught the basic language of corruption and deceit
Used as a hostage in their petty rows
Abuse of a child is not reviled in the marriage vows
So thrown against the fridge in silence he looks
At violence and pain unknown in his kiddies story books
Now they've traded the dummy for the TV
The teacher asks him what he wants to be
He never mentions a job on the factory floor
But then neither did his father some thirty years before
With dreams scraped from the TV screen
And a start in life best forgot
In this land of equal opportunity
What chance has he really got?

The Poem I Hope I Shall Never Write Called England

The poem I hope I shall never write called Engalnd, has 60
million pairs of sensible shoes, written in co-ordinated
pastels, it smiles a Dale Carnegie smile between the lines of
500 miles of dark blue pinstripes.

With a meal ticket for the gravy train you pay 6 Hail Mary's
and say you are just trying to get through, but is it ever
enough just to get through?

Dehumanised by the doberman mentality, behind the turrets of
the neighbourhood watch, I see the dust on the lustre of the
Emerald Isle and small swastikas on the latest liberty prints.
To the court of St James - never mind the product feel the
lifestyle. The writing on the wall bids you welcome to Hotel
Earth where as precious as poetry you hold up your life to the
light and find it ornate like a hollow vase or a pale thin
complexion, until shards of conscience kick sand in your suntan
lotion and you suffer with all the political depth of a
designer sweatshirt. It's the gospel according to St Michael
carrier bags. I breathe in - Whig history and the uncivil list,
Cathedral cities wringing their hands, invisible earnings and
the bank of opinion tells me throw another miner on the
barbecue.

Meanwhile..............

back at reality...............
                    the divisions blister

I see old men asking for ten pence outside multi-million pound
shopping centres, cardboard box bedouins bowing to the power of
the rota blades, bamboo Babel and the American wet dream.
Diluting to taste, Gazza attempts the futility of the Sun
crossword, I drank the world T shirt, unzips a grin, draws a
Hitler moustache on a Harrier jump jet, Benny Hill burgers for
breakfast, going down for the third time, sucking plankton, I
breathe in - Bingo culture, Smallville UK, Mr wet underpants 1989,
Death Valley Amusements and 10 pints of frogspawn. To the
court of St James - there's a view from any train pulling through
the backstreets of any Northern town calling you liar.
By the tomb of the unknown shopper another lorry dumps 2 tons
of ear wax on the wrong lawn and a fat tongue comes on the
radio, it says 'sorry but....sorry but...sorry but...(click)'.

At the end of your clean clothes chain in Anorak, tank top,
shorts and odd socks, on the way to the launderette you say
you're just trying to get through, but is it ever enough just
to get through? To the court of St James - there's blood on
your pages. I can almost see the stains on the white white
cliffs as we near the coast of the poem I hope I shall never
write called England.

JOHN AGARD: Guyanese poet, performer and storyteller, sweetly styled "poetsonian" - expressing his "kinship with the satirical spirit and folky surrealism of the calypsonian". John Agard came to Britain in 1977 and was soon recognised as a special presence on the poetry scene. In 1982 his collection *Man to Pan* won the Casas de las Americas prize. His other published work includes *Mangoes and Bullets* (Pluto Press 1985), and *Lovelines for a Goat Born Lady* (Serpent's Tail 1990). His most recent collection is *Laughter is an Egg* (Puffin 1990), written for children of all ages.

PATIENCE AGBABI: Young Nigerian-British poet whose reputation grows with each performance. She is highly active on the performance poetry scene, on the women's cultural circuit and in the Federation of Worker Writers. Her work is a lyrical-sounding of questions of identity and reveals a musically inspired gift, taking cues from rap and dub, while her rhythms remain distinctly her own.

BRIDGIT BARD: Poet and performance artist, born in Glasgow, based in London, where she works in adult and community education teaching communications, from literacy to body language. She practises poetry as a physical activity, linking it always with dance and theatre in an experiential whole. She describes her work as being inspired by shamanistic and bardic traditions, which understands poetry as ritual and a power for personal and social transformation. She has performed all over the U.K. and her work is published in the Mandarin anthology *Common Thread* (1989).

NEIL BARTLETT: Chichester-born, London-based writer, performer, director and cultural historian. Neil Bartlett's work is a joyous exploration of gay identities and sensibilities. He is the author of the acclaimed plays *A Vision of Love Revealed in Sleep* and *Sarrasine*. His book on Oscar Wilde, *Who Was That Man?*, and his first novel, *Ready to Catch Him Should He Fall*, are both published by Serpent's Tail.

JEAN "BINTA" BREEZE: Jamaican poet, playwright, actress, dancer and choreographer who first came to Britain in the early '80's. Jean "Binta" Breeze originally broke through as a 'dub-poet' making appearances in music and literature events throughout the world. While she will always be a 'dub-poet' her work now extends to take in writing for stage and television, and explores all forms of a finely-tuned personal lyricism. Her published works include *Riddym Ravings* (Race Today 1988) and *Spring Cleaning* (Virago 1992). Her recorded work includes *Tracks* (LKJ Records 1990).

BELINDA BURTON: Nottingham-based performance poet who's been standing up to audiences all over the U.K. since the mid-'80's. She is especially well-known on the women's circuit but her reputation extends throughout the performance poetry and cabaret scenes. Her work combines caustic wit and cartoon parody with moments of telling intimacy, all timed and delivered to devastating effect.

PARMINDER CHADDA: Black Asian poet and folksinger, born in Kenya now based in London. She describes herself as having traced the 'diaspora samosa, from India to Africa to England'. A long-time member of the Asian Women's Writers Collective yet she has published little of her work to date, defining her role as a poet as being essentially social and orientated to community based situations, cultural and educational. She is a poet who sets out to be heard rather than published, and explains this as an expression of her working through Indian traditions of orature, embracing storytelling, song and dance, but also as a reaction against the educational processing of literature. She speaks and sings in Punjabi, Hindi and English.

DEBJANI CHATTERJEE: Born in India and grew up in Japan, Hong Kong, Egypt and in the U.K.. Her poetry, stories and articles have been widely published and her two collections of poetry to date are *I Was That Woman* (Hippopotamus Press 1989) and *The Sun Rises in the North* (Smith Doorstop 1991). Her new collection is due out at any moment from Enitharmon. Her work displays the rare unison of a sharp eye and a fine ear and is shot-through with the rainbow spirit which lights up her life. She is the Director of Community Relations for Sheffield City Council and is a member of the Asian Women's Writers Collective.

MAYA CHOWDHRY: Glasgow-born, Sheffield-based writer, film-maker and photographer working "across, through and over" these artforms. She has written for T.V. and radio and her work has been published in a wide range of anthologies and magazines. She is a member of the

Asian Women's Writers Collective and is active as a literary animateur in the community. Her most recent performances have seen and heard her working with/against a backdrop of her own photographic images.

BRENDAN CLEARY: Born in County Antrim, Northern Ireland. He now lives in Newcastle where he works as a part-time lecturer, performance poet and stand-up comic. He is the editor of the essential small press magazine The Echo Room and through the late '80's organised the Morden Tower poetry events. He has published several pamphlets of poetry, including *Late Night Bouts* (Bad Seed Press 1987), *Memo's to Sensitive Eddie* (The Wide Skirt 1987), and *Newcastle is Benidorm* (Echo Room 1988). A full-length collection, *Whitebread & ITV*, was published in 1990 by The Wide Skirt. His work often deals with the raw realities, disillusion in love, politics, life on the skid - he often touches bottom, but usually finds a footing sure enough to push up on.

BOB COBBING: Internationally acclaimed sound/concrete poet. His work is a continual creative challenge to restrictive notions of the constitution of poetry. He has worked with many vocal/instrumental improvisatory groups including Bow Gamelan, Oral Complex, Random Access, and Bird Yak. His collected works appear in 13+ volumes published by small presses in the U.K., Canada and the U.S., and he has produced numerous records and tapes in no less than 9 countries. For many years he has been the coordinator of the Association of Little Presses and runs his own small press, Writers Forum.

MERLE COLLINS: Grenadian poet, performer and storywriter/teller. Her first novel, *Angel*, and collection of short stories, *Rain Darling*, are published by the Women's Press. Her first collection of poetry, *Because The Dawn Breaks*, was published in 1985 by Karia Press. Her new collection of poetry, *Rotten Pomerack*, is due out from Virago. Merle Collins is also widely known for her spellbinding performances, both solo and with the orature and music ensemble The African Dawn, with whom she has recorded two albums.

JAYNE CORTEZ: Internationally acclaimed African-American jazz-poet whose presence has been felt in the U.K. since the publication of her book *Coagulations* (Pluto Press 1984) and through her many memorable public performances here. She has developed a style of startling

POETS' PROFILES

technical virtuosity, of such visual and musical intensity that her texts demand vocal expression, and their impact is nothing short of physical. She has published several books and recordings of her work, the most recent being *Everywhere Drums* (book and album, both Bola Press 1991).

PETER FINCH: Experimental poet and performer, born in Cardiff where he still lives. Peter Finch avails himself of all compositional methods and materials - from familiar modes to techniques as varied as collage and cut-up, permutational and computer processes, to create a startling array of textual, visual, sound and tactile forms. His work continually extends the poetic licence - with nerve, nous and not a little humour. His published work includes *Selected Poems* (1987) and *poems for ghosts* (1991), both from Poetry Wales Press.

JOYOTI GRECH: She writes: "I was born in Dhaka, Bangladesh in 1963 when it was still part of Eastern Pakistan, the first daughter of a Maltese father and a mother from the Buddhist Chakma community of the country's southern hill region. My experience has taught me the fluidity of culture and the absurdity of nationality. As a Blackwoman living in England I have come to know the necessity of struggle, change, and an identity born of shared politics and vision. Imagination, fierce determination and tenderness build home wherever we go. Often we have to carry it with us". Joyoti Grech is a member of the Asian Women's Writers Collective.

JOHN HEGLEY: 'Poedian' and Poptician; one of the most original and popular figures to come through the Alternative Comedy scene. Whether deflating affectation or teasing meaning out of trivia, piling on the word-play or paring it down to the bone, John Hegley's poetry is as vital as it is excrutiatingly funny. He performs all over the U.K. and appears regularly on T.V. and radio. His first collections, all home made, have now been revised, enlarged and properly published, including *Glad To Wear Glasses* (Andre Deutsch 1990) and *Can I Come Down Now Dad?* (Methuen 1991). His poetry is also regularly featured in The Guardian.

ESSEX HEMPHILL: African-American gay poet and cultural activist, especially known to British audiences through his tours of 1986 and 1992. His work gives full expression to personal and relational realities both within the black gay and across the wider community, delivering a deeply evocative, proudly sexy and always affirmative vision. His collections include *Earth Life* and *Conditions* (Bebop Books 1985 and 1986) and his work appears in a number of anthologies published and/or available in the U.K., including *In The Life* (1986), *Tongues Untied* (GMP 1987), *High Risk* (Serpent's Tail 1991), and *Brother to Brother* (Alyson Pbcs. 1991) which he also edited. His work is also featured in the Isaac Julien film *Looking for Langston*.

JADE: Born in New Zealand, based in London. She writes: "I fell into poetry in my mid-twenties at roughly the same time as I fell out of my comfortably rebellious labels. Poetry has been my way of exploring the grey areas, the contradictions of who I am and how I experience the world." Highly active in the performance poetry scene, she is also published in *Language of Water*, *Language of Fire* (Oscars Press 1992), *Square Peg* magazine, and *Finding the Lesbians* (Crossing 1990).

KEITH JAFRATE: Grew up in Southall and now lives in Huddersfield where he is highly active in the burgeoning Yorkshire poetry scene. He is especially well known for his collaborations as a poet and saxophonist with jazz bands, producing an exciting new strain of jazz-poetry, with the rhythms serving meditative movements scored with vivid imagery. Keith Jafrate has also published several pamphlets through the small press scene including *War Poems* (Slow Dancer 1987) *Jump!* (Slow Dancer 1988) and *The Flame* (Purple Heather 1988).

LINTON KWESI JOHNSON: Poet, recording artist and political activist, born in Jamaica, he came to England in 1963. His work stands as historical testimony to the Black British experience. From the albums *Dread Beat An' Blood* and *Forces of Victory* in the '70's, *Bass Culture* and *Making History* in the '80's to *Tings an Times* in 1991 (the album published by Sterns, the book by Bloodaxe): from the man who minted Nation Language and coined the 'dub-poetry' movement - fusing reggae-rhythms, grass-roots realism and a critical global vision - a phenomenal body of work comes into ever clearer focus.

JOOLZ: Poet and raconteur, born and based in Bradford. Joolz is an original spark of the current popular poetry movement. Of the first generation punk-poets she has usually been associated with 'the ranters', whose rock-driven style her work parallelled before tracing its own trajectory. Her poems, stories and monologues explore the tension between the comedy and tragedy of

Poets' Profiles

people's lives, often speaking of the delusion and soon succeeding disillusion of working-class youth, to which her outrageous wit is a natural and necessary antidote. Joolz has performed her work throughout Britain, Europe and North America. To date she has published two collections *Mad, Bad & Dangerous to Know* (Virgin 1986) and *Emotional Terrorism* (Bloodaxe 1990). She has also recorded numerous albums and singles with musicians ranging from Jah Wobble to New Model Army.

JACKIE KAY: Poet and playwright, born in Edinburgh and brought up in Glasgow. Her work is a remarkable coalescence of the personal and political, a nexus of race, class, gender and sexuality. She writes in many voices and from a wide range of viewpoints and is always true to her experience of urban working-class realities. Her plays include *Chiaroscuro*, presented by the Theatre of Black Women in '86, and *Twice Over* presented by Gay Sweatshop in '88. Her T.V. work includes films on pornography, AIDS and transracial adoption. She was also a contributor to the BBC 2 Commissions and Collaborations season. Her poetry has been widely anthologised and her first collection, *The Adoption Papers*, was published in 1991 by Bloodaxe.

LINDA KING: Florida-born, now settled in London. Linda King has long been active in anti-racist and community arts work. She is a Black lesbian poet who confronts social and political issues with passion and dignity. Her work has been anthologised by Sheba and Virago. Against a strong performance and multi-media arts background, her recent work sees her developing a distinct jazz-blues poetry style. Working with many of the jazz scene's most prominent women musicians, this has culminated in the jazz-poetry band "Firebird".

TOM LEONARD: Born in Glasgow, where he still lives, Tom Leonard writes in both Glaswegian dialect and 'standard English', exploring working-class experience especially where it rubs up against institutionalised culture. His mode ranges between tender lyricism and savage satire. His books of poetry include *Intimate Voices* (Poems 1966-83), *Situations Theoretical and Contemporary* (1986) and *Nora's Place* (1990), all published by Galloping Dog.

LIZ LOCHHEAD: Born in Motherwell, based in Glasgow, a poet who naturally crosses over into theatre and cabaret. Her work is both funny and fierce and is especially concerned with sexu-

230

al politics and cultural identity. She is a hugely popular performer. Her publications include *Dreaming Frankenstein* (1984), *True Confessions*, a collection of her performance pieces, lyrics, raps and monologues (1985), both from Polygon, and *Bagpipe Muzak* (Penguin 1991). Her plays include *Mary Queen of Scots Got Her Head Chopped Off*, *Dracula, Blood and Ice*, *Same Difference*, and *Them Through The Wall*.

ABDUL MALIK: Born in Grenada, he grew up in Trinidad and Grenada where in the '60's he was involved in the Black Power Movement and became a Muslim, out of which experience he began composing and performing poetry. He became very well known for his performances at The Little Caribbean Theatre which involved drum and steel band accompaniments. He first performed in Britain in 1983 where he now lives. His collections include *The Whirlwind*, published by Panrun 1988, who have also published a recording of his work, *More Damned Power*.

MARC MATTHEWS: Guyanese poet, actor, film-maker and producer, now based in London. His work is a well-spring of the Caribbean oral tradition and draws deeply on Amerindian, African and European sources in creating new language forms and feelings, which he refers to as 'oralography'. An original member of the performance poetry groups Dem Two and All Ah We, and most recently in the U.K., He & She. His most recent publication is *Guyana, My Altar* (1987 Karnak House). A new title, *A Season of Sometimes* (Peepal Press) is due out soon.

MÁIGHRÉAD MEDBH: Performance poet, born in Newcastle West, she now lives in Dublin. Her work is a unique blend of lyrical sensuality and rhetorical toughness, charting her own growth and awakening, explicitly questioning the suppressive roles of the church and state, and celebrating an emerging sense of personal and political freedom. Strongly influenced by rock, reggae and rap, which provide the rhythmical frameworks for much of her poetry, she performs solo and with bands at various venues in Ireland. Her first collection, *The Making of a Pagan*, was published in 1990 by Blackstaff Press.

IAN McMILLAN: Poet, playmaker and broadcaster, born in Barnsley, South Yorkshire where he still lives. His poetry is characterised by a serious and sensitive wit and is a continual reminder of the unusual nature of everyday life. He performs his work in venues and schools all across the

U.K., is highly active in the small press scene, a founder of the Versewagon Mobile Writers Workshop and the poetry-cabaret group The Circus of Poets. His published work includes, *The Selected Poems* (Carcanet 1987), *The Unselected Poems* (The Wide Skirt 1988), *More Poems, Please, Waiter, And Quickly* (Sow's Ear Press 1989), and *A Chin?* (The Wide Skirt 1991).

HAJI-MIKE: London based Greek-Cypriot rapper and vrakamuffin-freek selector. He first began to experiment with poetry and music as a DJ in the late '70's and from then to now has developed highly original concepts and fusions, with the prime objectives of putting Cyprus and Cypriots on the cultural map and broadening the parameters of rap-poetry. He works both solo and with his band, Boudoum, which he describes as a "cultural saladin - where Greek meets reggae meets funk with a touch of jazz and rap".

ADRIAN MITCHELL: Poet, playwright and novelist, born and based in London. He is one of the pioneers in the contemporary popular poetry movement, and his performances, solo and with musicians all over the U.K., have moved hearts, minds and feet. His achievement in popularising poetry, in extending its reference and appeal and demonstrating its potential as a force of change in people's lives becomes ever more apparent. His books of poetry include *For Beauty Douglas: Collected Poems* (A&B 1982), *On The Beach At Cambridge* (A&B 1984), *Love Songs of World War Three* (A&B/WH Allen 1989), and *Greatest Hits* (Bloodaxe 1991).

GERALDINE MONK: Born in Blackburn, based in Sheffield, Geraldine Monk's intimate and experimental engagement with language has pushed poetry to pictorial and musical extremes; revelling in its structures and textures to reveal new properties and potentials. Her work has appeared in a wide range of magazines and anthologies in the U.K., France and the U.S.. Her publications, all small press, include *Tiger Lilies* (Rivelin 1982), *Herein Lie Tales of Two Cities* (Writers Forum 1986), *Sky Scapers* (Galloping Dog 1986), *Quaquaversals* (Writers Forum 1990), and *Outcasts and Inscapes* (forthcoming from Creation Press).

SISTER NETIFA: Poet, community worker, promoter and craftswoman, Sister Netifa lives and works in Notting Hill, London, where she runs the Uprising Culture House. A formidable and inspiring presence, her poetry is strongly influenced by dub and rapso styles and is an assertion of her identity as a working-class Black woman. She has performed her work throughout the U.K., Europe, North America and the Caribbean, both solo and with her band, the rootsical-reggae, all women Determined Band, with whom she has made two albums to date, the latest being *I Am A Poem* (1991). Her printed work includes *A Woman Determined,* published by Research Associates School Times Publications 1987.

GRACE NICHOLS: Born in Guyana, she came to Britain in 1977. Grace Nichols is a poet for whom the written and spoken word became the medium through which she re-established contact with her ancestral community, whose histories and mythologies she traces from the Caribbean to Africa through to the Americas, Asia and Europe, providing the substance and wide perspectives of her work. On another but always related level, she celebrates a physical and spiritual whole-someness that is the key to personal and political integrity. Writing in both English and Creole she delights in their constant interaction and perceives poetry as a radical synthesising force. Her collections of poetry include *i is a long memoried woman* (Karnak House 1983), *The Fat Black Woman's Poems* (Virago 1984), and *Lazy Thoughts of a Lazy Woman* (Virago 1989).

BROTHER NIYI: Nigerian-British, London-based poet and performer, mixing it up with dub, rap and jazz to produce a potent lyrical cocktail. Altogether a public poet, he has worked on a huge range of platforms, from the local community centre to the large scale theatre. His work has resulted in a number of artistic collaborations with both musicians and film-makers, including The African Dawn, DJ MC^2 and the techno-dance outfit Beatmasters, some of which has been committed to vinyl.

HENRY NORMAL: Manchester-based poet and humourist, variously described as 'urban romantic', 'nerd triumphant', 'enfant terrible of alternative poetry'. His themes centre around rela-tionships, especially the failures of modern love, and working-class culture and consciousness, depicting in both tragic and comic situations the encounter of idealism and cynicism. He works by parody and pastiche but also reveals an original and uncanny imaginative gift that leaves audi-ences thoroughly amused. Henry Normal is widely renowned for his live performances and T.V. appearances. He has also published a number of collections including *Is Love Science Fiction?* (1986), *Love Like Hell* (1988), *Does Inflation Affect the Emotions?* (1989), *A More Intimate*

Fame (1990) - all Twist in the Tail Productions, and *The Fifteenth of February* (Sheffield Popular Publishing 1992).

PITIKA NTULI: Poet, visual artist and teacher, born in Azania, he came to London in 1980 from the frontline of the struggle against the Apartheid state. He spent a year in a death row cell in Swaziland before international pressure secured his release into exile. His work as a poet is indivisible from his other artistic activities, which all explore the relationship between art, culture and politics. His work is both witty and deadly serious, sensuous and conceptual. On the page, as in his performances, he simultaneously entertains and challenges, engaging people in a process of radical creativity. He has performed and exhibited his work all over the U.K., Europe, North America and Africa.

MARSHA PRESCOD: Trinidadian-born, London-based poet and story-writer whose work first found an audience in the early '80's. A popular performer, her work sparkles with a satirical intelligence and a strong musical sensibility. Widely anthologised, her major collection to date, *Land of Rope and Tory*, was published by Akira Press.

BROTHER RESISTANCE: Poet, performance and recording artist, born Trinidad and Tobago, between where and London he shares his time. He is the founding member of the Network Community Organisation and the Network Riddum Band of which he is the resident poet, and whose work has led to the development of a new progression of poetry called RAPSO. Rapso is founded on a network of vocal and percussive rhythms, principally those of the African drum and Steel pan. Rapso has its historical roots in the ancient African tradition of the Griot, of the itinerant, community poet, philosopher and historian. Rapso is living street theatre. To date Brother Resistance has released over 4 albums with the Network Riddum Band, and his major publication in the U.K., *Rapso Explosion*, appeared in 1986 from Karia Press.

AHMED SHEIKH: Senegalese poet and cultural worker, exiled in London. He is a founder member of the African Dawn orature and music ensemble with whom he produced four albums, including *Conversation* (1984), *Chimurenga* (1987) and *Jali* (1989). He is also a founder member of Artrage magazine and is active on the Africa Centre programming committee.

His poetry and articles are widely published. He is the author of *David M. Diop: The Aesthetics of Liberation*. His poetry achieves a rare synthesis between explicitly political content and natural lyrical grace.

LEMN SISSAY: Poet, playwright and vocalist with the jazz-funk fusion band Secret Society. The full force of his work has been felt by audiences all over the U.K. and Europe. A dramatic and engaging performer his work explores what it means to be Black and British, exposes social/cultural cant, confronts chauvinistic forces with anger but also with humour and humanity, and always celebrates the liberating power of the spoken and written word. His collections of poetry include *Tender Fingers in a Clenched Fist* (Bogle L'Ouverture 1988) and *Rebel Without Applause* (Bloodaxe 1992). His recordings include *Black Vibe* (Bebop Cassettes 1989), and *Live and Unleashed* (1990).

CHERRY SMYTH: 'Upfront lesbian poet', fiction writer and journalist who openly takes risks in her work to stimulate dialogues around taboo subjects, especially women's sexuality, about which she writes with explicit honesty. Her creative and journalistic work represents a serious challenge to both prejudice and naivety. Her poetry and fiction have appeared in a wide range of anthologies and periodicals, including *Serious Pleasure* and *More Serious Pleasure* (Sheba 1988 & 1990), and *Seeing in the Dark* (Serpent's Tail 1990). Her journalistic work is also widely published, some of it collected in the publication *Lesbians Talk Queer Notions* (Scarlett Press 1982). She is the 'Out' editor of City Limits magazine. She is Irish and lives in London.

NEIL SPARKES: Poet, musician and painter, fast filling-out uniquely conceived forms of jazz/blues poetry. His work is coloured by high-grade urban realism and a survivor's wit, and patterned by strong rhythmical movements. His publications include *All Metal and Other Men's Wives* (1989) and *Rumba Rumba* (1990) both published by Hangman Books. His performance projects include collaborations with some of the most prominent jazz-musicians in the U.K., for example Dick Heckstall-Smith and Brian Abrahams in the jazz-poetry ensemble Rhythm 'n' Ink.

ATTILA THE STOCKBROKER: Poet/songwriter who gate-crashed the culture in the early '80's with the wave of punk-poets collectively known as 'the ranters'. Often accompanied by thrash mandola, his work is streaked through with rhetorical realism and riotous humour, all riding on strong rock-rhythms. His albums include *Ranting at the Nation* (1983), *Sawdust and Empire* (1984), *Lybian Students from Hell* (1987), *Scornflakes* (1988) and *Donkey's Years* (1991). His latest book *668 Neighbour of the Beast* is due out from Bloodaxe in 1992. He has performed his work all over the U.K., Europe, North America and Australia.

LEVI TAFARI: Liverpool-based dub-poet and 'urban griot'. His work is informed by the rhythms of reggae and its musical foundation has lead him to perform with a number of bands, including the Delado Drum and Dance Group, The Ministry of Love, and Urban Strawberry Lunch. His work has appeared in a wide range of anthologies and magazines and on a number of recordings, released for example through Zulu Records and Midnight Music. His collections in print include *Duboetry* (Merseyside Poetry 1988). A hard-hitting and highly entertaining performer, he has made numerous appearances on T.V., not least as the resident poet on the Grange Hill schools T.V. series.

ELEAN THOMAS: Jamaican poet, novelist and political/cultural worker. She lived in England from the mid '80's to the early '90's, in which period she published two collections of poetry, *Word Rhythms* and *Before They Can Speak of Flowers* (both Karia Press), and her first novel, The Last Room (published by Virago). Her work is a celebration of struggle on all fronts - race, gender, class - and ultimately a vision of one world.

NICK TOCZEK: Poet, promoter, lecturer, political researcher and journalist. He has published over a dozen books of poetry and creative writing, his most recent being *The Private Crimes of Nick Toczek* (Amazing Colossal Press 1989) and his collected performance poems, *The Meat Boutique* (PBB 1991). He has also released several albums and cassettes with a number of rock bands, including *Intoczekating* (1987) and *Britanarchists* (1986), both on Acrimony Records. His work takes on sensitive social and overtly political issues and works away from simplistic moral positions. An exciting and visual performer he delights in the physical properties of language, building-up sound-textures within a poem that render it almost palpable.

STORME WEBBER: African-American poet and performer who has been living and working in the U.K. for the best part of the last three years. Her work as a poet brings together all elements of a strong performing arts background, incorporating theatre, dance and song in a seamless unity. Her poetry is especially felt for its sensuous engagement with themes of personal and social liberation, in particular her identity and experience as an African-American lesbian. She is the author of *Diaspora*, a collection of poetry and graphics, and her work was heavily featured in Sheba's *Serious Pleasure* and *More Serious Pleasure* publications (1988 & 1990).

AARON WILLIAMSON: Brighton-based experimental poet and performer. His books include *Liberty, Freedom & Tinsel* (1989) and *Cathedral Lung* (1992) both published by Creation Press. His work exhibits a breathtaking linguistic exuberance offset by intense dramatic realisation. He is profoundly deaf and has evolved a physical approach to demonstrating a text in performance, creating an ecstatic and often unnerving sound-spectacle.

BENJAMIN ZEPHANIAH: Dub-poet and playwright, born in Birmingham, based in London. He broke through on the cabaret and performance poetry circuits of the early '80's and the poetry world has never been the same since. His work, fashioned in English and Jamaican patois, is a potent mix of critical wit and extraordinary verbal agility, and serves a generous and uncompromising vision. He has performed his work world-wide, cultivating artistic and political alliances across continents. His books include *The Dread Affair* (Arena 1985), *Inna Liverpool* (Africa Arts Collective 1990), *Rasta Time in Palestine* (Shakti 1991), and *City Psalms* (Bloodaxe 1992). His albums include *Dub Ranting*, *Rasta* and *Us an Dem* (released in 1990 from Island/Mango).

ANN ZIETY: Performance poet and writer, born in Manchester, based in London. She writes in a range of styles, from fine-spun lyrical meditations to expansive satirical rants. A popular performer of her work, she has appeared in venues all over the U.K.. Her poetry and short stories have been published in anthologies by Sheba, Pandora and Virago.

Apples & Snakes would like to thank all the poets for permission to include their work in this anthology. We would also like to acknowledge the following publishers as the first source of individual texts:

Virago Press for Red Rebel Woman by Jean "Binta" Breeze (Spring Cleaning 1992); Penguin Books for Bagpipe Muzak and View of Scotland by Liz Lochhead (Bagpipe Muzak 1991); Bloodaxe for Dressing Up and Dance of the Cherry Blossom by Jackie Kay (The Adoption Papers 1991); Bogle L'Ouverture for The Show Goes On by Lemn Sissay (Tender Fingers 1988) and Smith Doorstop for Bearing Witness and Boiling Up (The Sun Rises in the North 1991); Bloodaxe/LKJ for Di Anfinish Revalueshan by Linton Kwesi Johnson (Tings an Times 1991); Allison & Busby for Evenings of Fire and Snow by Adrian Mitchell (Love Songs of World War Three 1989); Pluto Press, Serpent's Tail and Greenheart for Heart Transplant, In Times of Love and Limbo Dancer's Memo by John Agard (Mangoes & Bullets 1985, Love Lines 1990 and Limbo Dancer in Dark Glasses 1983); Karnack House for U Freak Out by Marc Matthews (Guyana, My Altar 1987); Harry's Hand and The Wide Skirt for The Er Barnsley Seascape and Elvis is Ted Hughes by Ian McMillan (1989 & 1991); Poetry Wales Press/Siren for Dribble Creeps and Hills by Peter Finch (poems for ghosts 1991); Label Magazine for Departure by Geraldine Monk (1988); Creation Press for the Freedom, Liberty & Tinsel extract by Aaron Williamson (Cathedral Lung 1992); Slow Dancer for Acappella by Keith Jafrate (Jump! 1988); Stand Magazine for Slouch by Brendan Cleary (1990); Gay Men's Press and Alyson Publications for Skin Catch Fire and Commitments by Essex Hemphill (Tongues Untied 1987 and Brother to Brother 1992); Hippopotamus Press for Primary Purpose by Debjani Chatterjee (I Was That Woman 1989); PBB for Financial Affairs by Nick Toczek (Meat Boutique 1991); Karia Press for The Tourist by Elean Thomas (Before They Can Speak of Flowers 1990); Bola Press for What's Happening and Push Back the Catastrophes by Jayne Cortez (Everywhere Drums 1991); Label and Pandora Press for On the Darker Side of the Flyover and The Outrage by Ann Ziety (1988 & 1989); Twist in the Tail and Sheffield Popular Publishing for This Land of Equal Opportunities, The Poem I Hope I Shall Never Write Called England, and Ostrich Man by Henry Normal (A More Intimate Fame 1990 and The Fifteenth of February 1992).

Apples & Snakes would like to express special thanks to the huge number of individuals, groups and organisations who have contributed to its programme and development, including:

Ruth Harrison, Lolita Ratchford, Wendy Metcalf, Debra Serrant, Mel Steel, Pitika Ntuli, Sonita Alleyne, Mandy Williams, Netifa Akousa, Bicca Maseko, Niyi Onilude, Gail Thompson, Karin Woodley, Tony Gifford, Ken Worpole, Jacob Ross, Chantal Benjamin, Roy McKenzie, June Reid, Sue Sinclair, Chris Cardale, Dennis Robinson, Steve Lobb, Bernie Cunnane, Pete Murray, Adrian Gennard, Karl Birjucov, Bruce Barnes, Dirg Aarb-Richards, Laurence Bayliss, Bramwell Osula, Lavinia Greenlaw, Sue Bowers, Hannah Wilmot, Maggie Pinhorn, Antonia Byatt, Kerwin Doctrové, Mark Wilbur, Kwesi Owusu, Mahmood Jamal, Val Bloom, Fred Williams, Martin Glynn, J.D. Douglas, Desmond Johnson, Sista Culcha, Lynford French, Lioness Chant, Leonora Rogers-Wright, Subi Shah, Lindsay McRae, Trisha Lee, Ferenc Aszmann, Steven Wells, John Cooper Clarke, Brian Patten, Roger McGough, Michael Rosen, Ivor Cutler, Fran Landesman, Michael Horovitz, Cecil Rajendra, Eric Huntley, Jessica Huntley, Sujata Bhatt, Marg Yeo, June Jordan, Lawrence Ferlinghetti, Shake Keane, Jalal Nuriddin, Oku Onuoro, Galliano, MC Mello, Marxman, Paul Bradshaw, Gilles Peterson, Jez Nelson, Lol Coxhill, Maggie Nicols, Carol Grimes, Mervyn Africa, Bukky Leo, Brian Abrahams, Ian Shaw, Jan Ponsford, Frank Williams, Jean Toussaint, Billy Jenkins, Talvin Singh, Inder Matharu, Keith Waithe, Jackson Sloan, Annie Whitehead, Cheryl Alleyne, Juwon Ogungbe, Dick Heckstall-Smith, Paul Rogers, Janette Mason, Louise Elliot, Laka Daisical, Tunde Jegede, Pinise Saul, Shikisha, Jungr & Parker, Some Like It Hot, The Well Oiled Sisters, Julie McNamara, Clea & McLeod, Rory McLeod, Kevin Seisay, The Chuffinelles, Janice Perry, Claire Dowie, Pat Condell, Mark Hurst, Logan Murray, Phillip Jupitus, Sheila Hyde, Curtis & Ishmael, Mr Nasty, Linda Smith, Skint Video, Tymon Dogg, Vi Subversa, Viv Acious, Sensible Footwear, Munirah, The Dinner Ladies, the Federation of Worker Writers, the Asian Women's Writers Collective, Spare Rib, London Disability Arts Forum, Kate O'Reilly, Sarah Scott, Bushy Kelly, Survivor Poets, The Oscars, Alison Russell, Pete Read, all our friends and colleagues in every part of the U.K. with whom we've worked through the years, thanks.